BECOMING YOUR HUSBAND'S

Mistress

...a woman without competition

Dee Johnson, LCSW

www.FacingForwardOnline.org

To Samina
We have a job to do
Lets do it well

[signature] LCSW
10/2014

Becoming Your Husband's Mistress

This book is designed to provide accurate and authoritative information with regard to the subject matter covered. This information is given with the understanding that the author is not engaged in rendering legal or professional advice. Since the details of your situation are fact dependent, you should additionally seek the services of a competent professional.

Published by Dee Johnson, LCSW

Dedication

I would like to dedicate this to my wonderful, supportive husband, Mr. Earnest E. Johnson Jr.

Thank you for allowing me to be your wife and life partner.

I promise to make it my mission to always be your mistress!

Acknowledgements

I want to acknowledge a wonderful, loving, faithful God who has chosen me as His vessel to get His message of unconditional love and acceptance out to the world. Without you God, there would be no me.

I want to acknowledge my 2 wonderful children, Jonathan and Jason. Thank you for allowing me time to do God's work and thank you for allowing me to be your mom. Both of you make me proud everyday and words cannot express the depth of my love towards you.

I want to acknowledge all of the women that give me inspiration for the work that I do.

And I want to acknowledge every married mistress and every future married mistress. We've got a job to ladies. So let's do it well!

Table of Contents

Preface

[1] "Mistress: A mysterious sexy woman that a married man sees in secret to have a romantic and sexual relationship with. This is the definition of a mistress. There is good sex, hotel room adventures, late nights, seductive phone calls, exciting secret dates, gifts and the thrill of doing something bad. The mistress holds all the power. She is the one who has the married man under a love spell and she gets all his attention and time that he should be spending with his wife. She is the one he fantasizes about when he is with his wife and the one he misses. He urges for her company and longs to hear her voice. The mistress is the woman a married man makes first priority and will shower her with gifts to keep her happy."

Introduction

Television shows, movies and soap operas all play a part in the development of our ideas regarding marriage. The Huxtables, the Waltons and the Bradys have been the married couples portrayed to show us how marriages work, how to resolve conflicts, and how to successfully navigate difficult circumstances. But what these married TV couples don't show us is how to deal successfully with difficult spouses who bring a host of issues into the marriage that we are too ill-equipped to handle. Issues such as spiritual immaturity, financial irresponsibility and sexual promiscuity that plague a marriage and threaten to destroy it are things that we wives never expected to face once we exchanged wedding vows. And if we did expect those behaviors from our men we erroneously believed that we were capable of changing those negative behaviors once we took their last names.

And so we rush into marriage thinking that the majority of our problems will be solved once we get the title wife only to find out that the men we married are nothing like the men we dated. Naively, we get married thinking that love will be enough to help us conquer any challenge and prevail against any adversity we may face. And that is partially true. Love for our spouses can help us stay committed to see them through when difficult circumstances show up. But as we often find out, love is not all that is needed to make a marriage successful. And sometimes love is the polar opposite of our feelings towards our spouses when they have hurt or disappointed us. As a result of all of this, women are often faced with the difficult choice of whether to stay or to leave the relationship. If we stay, we have to look at and interact with this person who has done things to us that we could never have predicted. And if we go, we will have to face the pain and uncertainty of what the future holds and give up our dreams of having our happily ever after. And more times than not, most of us choose to stay. We stay because it's easier. We stay because we think that every man will act the same way so why try to get another man to make us happy. We stay because we don't want to disrupt our children's lives. We stay because we don't want to start over again. We stay and suffer in silence, not getting our needs met and unable to move forward in our relationships.

Let me say this to all of the wives that have experienced what I have just described. I have been there. I have suffered similar pains, faced the harsh reality of being disappointed by love and have had to weigh the pros and cons of whether to leave or to stay.

Many of us are allowing all of the hurts, disappointments and resentments in our relationships to keep us from becoming the type of wives and women that God created us to become. We have built up walls around our hearts in an effort to protect ourselves from getting hurt but what is really happening is that we are in lifeless marriages and not getting our needs met. The results of this are marital crisis and children and households in distress.

There is nothing like marriage to provide a dose of reality and wake us from our fairy tale dream.

But what God said to me about this issue is that it's time to put our hurts, disappointments and resentments on the altar so we can experience healing. We wives need to realize that we will never be fulfilled in our marital relationships if we refuse to DO SOMETHING DIFFERENT. Yes, the experiences of yesterday were painful. Yes, yesterday changed the course of our relationships forever. Yes, yesterday almost caused us to crumble. But there is nothing that can be done about yesterday. So we need to learn to stop camping out at yesterday's door. The yesterdays of life are simply meant to be a history lesson to give us wisdom concerning the future. The goal is to find the peace of today. In order to be at peace, we must learn the art of forgiveness.

Holding onto bitterness and harboring negative emotions about our husbands is unproductive because it does nothing to solve the offense that has been committed.

Negative emotions only keep us in bondage but mask itself to make it seem like we are in control.

Forgiveness is the key to freedom.

We can no longer afford to keep what is in our hands waiting to see if our husbands are worthy of it. If we do, we will always be unsatisfied and unfulfilled in our marital relationships. We need to free our husbands from the debt that we think they owe, so we ourselves may experience freedom and begin to experience marital bliss.

As I struggled in my relationship with my husband and remained unable to decide if I really wanted to give my marriage another chance, God began to minister to me. He began talking to me about changing the dynamic of our relationship. He encouraged me to think differently, behave differently, and present myself differently and to make it my mission to become the woman of my husband's dreams.

And what I realized is that we wives must learn to love our husbands completely-just as they are today, right now at this very moment, flaws and all. We must be willing to express the love we have in our hearts towards them even if we aren't sure that we will get anything in return.

But because we will be doing it freely and without expectations, we will always get a return on our investment because this type of unconditional love draws people in. When we sow love, we will get love back. When we sow appreciation and admiration, we will get that back. When we sow positive things, positive things will return to us. We will reap whatever we sow.

So instead of sitting and waiting, it's time to get up and sow. Sow seeds of kindness. Sow seeds of affection.

Sow seeds of love and respect. And watch what you get in return. If you want to be the wife of your husband's dreams, you need to freely express love towards him-- without expectation, without fear, and without reservation.

And while on my journey, I thought that if I was having so many difficulties in my marriage, then other wives were likely to be experiencing the same struggles. So I decided to document what I learned along the way. So this book is all about the experiences and the lessons that I have learned along the way concerning God, myself and relationships.

This book was written for wives and future wives who are at a loss on how to get the most from their relationships, for women who want to rekindle the spark and passion in their relationships and for women who are currently in the state of choosing whether or not to pack their bags and get the heck out of dodge.

Purpose

Before we begin let me say a few words about this journey.

First, if you want a book about how you can get your needs met in your marriage, this isn't it. This book is a no nonsense guide on what wives should be doing in their relationships to keep the home fires burning and to try to prevent husbands from seeking to get their needs met elsewhere. I will not talk about what your husband should be doing in the marriage. I will not focus on how to get him to change his behaviors. This book is only about you and me and the contributions we can make in our marriages as we strive for marital bliss. We will be taking a hard look at the many ways we each sabotage our relationships and things we can begin doing to become the woman that our husbands fantasize about. This book is solely about women. It will require you to work. It will require you to reflect. And it will require you to deal with yourself and the way you treat your husband. The work will challenge you to make changes so you can achieve the type of marriage you have always dreamed of.

Secondly, there will be references about God, the bible and Christian principles throughout this book. However, the primary focus is to offer practical advice on this subject matter. One of the things I dislike about most Christian self help books is that there are often so many bible verses and not enough "how to" information. If you share that same frustration, you will not be disappointed. I will not use biblical references without practical, real life methods on how to implement the changes into your life.

Thirdly, the heart of your husband may be completely turned from you. He may already be in a relationship with another woman or he could be physically present but emotionally absent. I am not claiming that the methods outlined in this book will cure all of your marital woes. I am saying that by adopting the methods outlined in this book you should begin seeing some positive changes in your relationship. Deeper hurts, resentments and regrets must be worked through to get to the root of the real issues that are plaguing your marriage. But until then, we will focus on what you can do to begin turning your relationship around and to create a safe environment for your husband to love you.

Fourth, the information in this book may not be applicable to every married man. Some men will cheat no matter what his wife does. That is a character issue that needs to be dealt with at the feet of Jesus and sometimes in front of a judge. The information outlined within is geared towards women who want to keep their marriages intact and attempt to keep their men happy and faithful.

Fifth, if you are saying to yourself "I thought this book was going to be about sex and seduction", don't worry, we will get to that. But since you do not spend the majority of your day in the bedroom, it is important that you deal with the issues outside of the bedroom first.

The mistress is not only sought after because of great sex. She is also desirable to men because of the way she makes them feel. So be patient. We will talk about sex later.

Lastly, most of the information contained in this book is based on my own personal experience as a wife. I am simply telling you about the mistakes I have made as a wife and outlining lessons that I have learned in my 12 year relationship with my husband. I am also including information that I have gathered as a therapist, friend, information from articles, the internet, surveys, and books. I am not claiming to be an expert because I am still on my journey. But I am claiming to be a woman committed to keeping my marriage and family intact.

The purpose of this book is to empower women to take another look at the role that they play in their marital relationships. It is time for us to get ourselves back into the game instead of allowing things to "just happen". No longer will we wives sit on the sidelines of our marriages and allow other women to seize on the opportunity to enter our relationships. We must stop playing the role of a victim and become an active participant in our own lives. We need to become intentional about our marital interactions, passionate about our martial purposes and consistent in communicating positively to our spouse. It is my hope that each woman reading this book will understand that she is powerful beyond her comprehension and can influence the world if she can positively influence those in her household. It is my prayer that every wife would make it her mission to become her husband's mistress.

My Story

When I began working on this project, I had already
filled out divorce papers, got a separate bank account,
and was actively searching for an affordable place
where I could move with my two sons. Needless to say,
I was completely done with the idea of being married.
At that point, my husband and I had been in a
relationship for 11 years, married for 7. We had
weathered many storms, mostly due to his
unwillingness to "get it together", in my opinion. I was
tired of being the housekeeper, bookkeeper, homework
checker, grocery shopper, laundry washer, nurse and
counselor in my household. Not to mention, also being
a lover when night fall came. I felt unappreciated, taken
advantage of and taken for granted. I was completely
exhausted and overwhelmed by my many roles while
also holding down a full time job. I had come to the
conclusion that if I had to juggle so many
responsibilities then I really didn't need a husband. And
so I began the process of separating myself from him
one day at a time. He would try to talk to me but I was
in no mood to listen. He would try to help out more but
I knew it would be short lived and that things would
return to the way they always did-with me stuck taking
care of everything. Then he took a new approach to get
my attention. He tried to blame me for our problems!
Was he serious? Did he have the nerve to say that this
mess was my fault and that the reason he didn't do
more was because of me? What a likely excuse! Blame
the person that is holding everything together. Of

course, he just proved to me that I was making the right decision by ending this unfulfilling relationship.

Then one day, on one of those rare occasions when I actually gave him my full attention and a listening ear, he said something that changed my perspective. He said that he didn't help out around the house more because he was afraid of my responses to him if things weren't done the way I wanted them done. He went on to say that no matter what he did for me, for the children or for the household, that I would criticize the way he did it, how long it took for him to do it, or how long it took him to realize that I needed help. He felt that he couldn't catch a break with me. He was tired of the smart remarks and sarcastic tone he received from me whenever he attempted to be helpful. So, he just stopped trying. Of course I tried to minimize my part and turn the tables back on him-just like I had always done in the past. This caused him to shut down and stop talking-just like he had always done in the past. And we were back to business as usual which means we were barely getting along, living like two people that just tolerated each other.

But as the days passed following my husband's comment about my treatment of him I began to take a long, hard look in the mirror and evaluate the type of wife I really was. And when I began to be honest with myself about myself, I began to see that I had a lot to do with the reasons why my marriage was in the shape that it was in.

The Revelation

I was the type of wife that found something to complain about no matter how good things were going in our relationship. If he did something that offended me or that I deemed inconsiderate, I would criticize and talk to him like he was a child instead of a grown man. If I told him that I forgave him for something, whenever it was convenient I would bring the incident up over and over again and make it relevant to our current situation. And some of those things were years old. I'm talking up to 10 years old. But I was very good at laying out a case about how the past bore resemblance to the present and how he was acting the exact same way he did back then.

I was pessimistic about everything but called myself a realist. I didn't want to participate in any activities that I did not find interesting even if my husband liked to do those things. I refused to be submissive because I was a published author, an independent woman with a Masters degree, many certifications and my own mind and didn't find it necessary to submit to my husband's leadership. I refused to be cooperative or even to compromise. Now there were times when I was loving, adoring, fun and kind but those times together paled in comparison to the many times that I criticized and disrespected my husband.

I would also get with my girlfriends and talk badly about him behind his back while they talked about how miserable their husbands made them. And while participating in that type of discussion in that type of negative atmosphere, I was unknowingly feeding my spirit negative emotions, feelings and thoughts about my husband. So when I returned home after one of those husband bashing sessions, there was no way to be loving and kind. What my husband got instead were more complaints, more looks of disgust, more contempt and less affection.

I did all of these things because I was waiting on my husband to change. He had some habits, ideas and beliefs that I didn't agree with so in my mind he didn't deserve respect from me. He would have to earn respect if he wanted it. And the more he tried the more faults I found with his attempts to make changes. And we were caught in this vicious cycle for 11 years before God finally showed me that I was largely responsible for the state of our relationship.

As I look back on it now, I am ashamed to have called myself a Christian. In fact, very few of the interactions that I had with my husband, resembled the life of Christ. I was the exact opposite of Christ. I was unforgiving, merciless, unkind and rude. I was judgmental, temperamental and touchy. If I had a bad day at work or sat in traffic for too long I would take my frustrations out on him. There was not a day that went by that I didn't complain about something no matter how big or small. During this time, I was teaching bible study classes on marriage and was studying God's word and knew what I was expected to do. I was sending out daily devotionals encouraging people to live a life that Christ would be proud of but I rarely sought God's help concerning the state of my marriage. I didn't think my husband deserved any better because he had not made the changes that I wanted from him. So I continued to justify my bad attitude and our marriage remained stagnant and experienced very little growth.

The other reason that I didn't seek God's help is because I thought I had what it took to change my marriage, myself, and my husband on my own. So I continued doing what I thought would change our marriage. I tried talking to my husband, threatening to leave him, manipulating him, crying to him about how miserable I was. I did everything I could think of to get him to change. And he would change for a little while but the changes were always short-lived. Things weren't all bad all of the time but our marriage didn't flourish as much as it should have considering the length of time we had been a couple. It wasn't until I got serious about writing this book that I began focusing on what I could do to change the course of the relationship.

The Turning Point

Around the same time of my revelation, I had just left a job working as a therapist in a juvenile detention center for males. And although I had only worked there for a few short months I distinctly remembered aspects about my former clients' lives that were really disturbing to me. In particular, I began thinking back to the one thing most of them all had in common-there was no father in their lives. As a matter of fact, there was only one teen whose father was involved and playing an active role in his son's life. When visitation time came, the waiting room was full of mothers. The stories that I heard time and time again from these clients was that their dads had left home and had forgotten that they had children. The dads had simply chosen not to be parents anymore. The consequences of their fathers' decisions were unresolved grief, misplaced anger, and sadness that were often expressed violently by their sons. And even though the evidence of fatherless sons was etched into my mind, I tried to dismiss it by telling myself if I ended my marriage that those things would never happen to my boys. They were being raised by a strong Christian mother who loved them wholeheartedly and they had several strong male figures in their lives they could look to for guidance on male issues. And even though I made a convincing argument to myself, I could not ignore the statistics. I was forced to consider the effects that a divorce could potentially have on our 2 boys, our babies, our little gifts from God.

According to Getting Men Involved: The Newsletter of the Bay Area Male Involvement Network, Spring 1997:

•63% of youth suicides are from fatherless homes (Source: U.S. D.H.H.S., Bureau of the Census)

•90% of all homeless and runaway children are from

fatherless homes

•85% of all children that exhibit behavioral disorders come from fatherless homes (Source: Center for Disease Control)

•80% of rapists motivated with displaced anger come from fatherless homes (Source: Criminal Justice & Behavior, Vol 14, p. 403-26, 1978.)

•71% of all high school dropouts come from fatherless homes (Source: National Principals Association Report on the State of High Schools.)

•75% of all adolescent patients in chemical abuse centers come from fatherless homes (Source: Rainbows for all Gods Children.)

•70% of juveniles in state-operated institutions come from fatherless homes (Source: U.S. Dept. of Justice, Special Report, Sept 1988)

•85% of all youths sitting in prisons grew up in a fatherless home (Source: Fulton Co. Georgia jail populations, Texas Dept. of Corrections 1992)

Other sources say:

- Children of divorce, particularly boys, tend to be more aggressive toward others than those children whose parents did not divorce. (Emery, Marriage, Divorce and Children's Adjustment, 1988)

- People who come from broken homes are almost

twice as likely to attempt suicide than those who do not come from broken homes. (Velez-Cohen, Suicidal Behavior and Ideation in a Community Sample of Children Journal of the American Academy of Child and Adolescent Psychiatry 1988)

- Children of divorced parents are roughly two times more likely to drop out of high school than their peers who benefit from living with parents who did not divorce. (McLanahan, Sandefur, Growing Up With a Single Parent: What Hurts, What Helps Harvard University Press 1994)

- Seventy percent of long-term prison inmates grew up in broken homes. (Horn, Bush, Fathers, Marriage and Welfare Reform)

I concluded that I wouldn't be able to live with myself if my children ever became a statistic because I had chosen to break up their family. I would never be able to justify that or find that acceptable. I had brought these two kids into the world and it was my responsibility to do everything in my power to ensure that they didn't have to experience the effects of coming from a broken home. As a parent, that was the least I could do for my children.

Additionally, I didn't want my marriage to end until I put forth my best efforts at saving it. I had a lot on the line if this marriage failed. As a therapist I have learned that a divorce is similar to losing someone to a death. There is a grieving period that one must go through. The person has to learn to life without their significant other in their lives. The children are affected. The finances are affected. Friendships are affected. That was way too much to have to deal with if I let my relationship end up in the marital graveyard.

Besides, my husband and I were setting an example of what a Christian marriage should look like. If we were dysfunctional in our relationship, then there was a high probability that our children would grow up and have dysfunctional relationships of their own. And I didn't want to be responsible for that happening. But I also didn't want to be the woman who waited until the children were grown and out of the house before I could enjoy my life. Fifteen more years was just too long to wait for happiness! If I was going to stay married, then I wanted to be happy, content and fulfilled. I realized that I had to put into the relationship what I wanted to get out of it. I concluded that if I was going to have a fulfilling relationship, then I would have to learn to make changes in the area that my husband complained about the most-my mouth. I would have to decide that instead of using my voice to be critical of my husband, I needed to use it to encourage, support and build him up. I would have to learn how to speak my husband's love language.

And so my journey began. I began my journey by changing myself. I began to make little changes day by day in the way that I talked to, interacted with and thought about my husband. I allowed myself to enjoy his company without expecting him to act a certain way or to say certain things.

Then God dropped a new concept into my spirit...***Becoming My Husband's Mistress!***

Almost immediately after I began this journey I began to see results. My husband made the comment that he didn't want to be the test dummy for my new book. But he also couldn't resist enjoying me and our relationship as I worked to please him. I just kept treating him the way that I wanted to be treated and within the first 2-3 weeks I noticed a difference. He began opening up and sharing his heart with me. He began to trust my intentions and began being more affectionate with me. I came to the conclusion that the reason that I saw such quick results was because I had finally become the woman he had always desired. He was waiting on the mistress to show up all along and he was eager for her time and attention. He began to feel safe. He began to feel like he was adequate because I began building him up and pointing out all of his good qualities. I no longer talked to him about what he was doing wrong but I began highlighting the many things he was doing right. I can't say that I got it right every day but I was consistent enough with my new approach that he began to desire me in a new way. I saw what a positive impact my new approach was having on him. It was bringing him closer to me, closer to our children and closer to God. He was spending more time at home and less time at work. He began helping out around the house more often. My unconditional love towards and acceptance of him began healing our relationship. And it began healing those wounds from his childhood and from his past relationships. That's when I knew that I had made the right decision to stay married.

Confirmation

Prior to implementing any changes, two things happened. First, my husband shared with me that a female vendor at his job had asked him to take her out to lunch. Now, this woman knew that my husband was a married man with children, yet she felt it was okay to ask him out on a date. I guess in this day and age that the way people act and think shouldn't surprise me but I was completely disgusted that a single woman would intentionally try to insert herself into the life of a married man. Who did she thinks she was? And why did she think it was okay to go after my husband? The thought of such a disrespectful action by another woman only strengthened my resolve to become the woman of my husband's dreams. (Isn't it funny that we don't want something until someone else tries to take it from us?) He may not have been perfect, but he was mine and I wasn't going to stand by while someone attempted to hurt the family that he and I had created. After he told me about the incident I realized that if I didn't change my ways quickly I was going to have a bigger fight on my hands.

Secondly, I ran across an article on the internet that was published about a mistress that proudly sleeps with married men. The woman had a website specifically for married people, both men and women, who wanted to have extramarital affairs. The website boasts having over 650,000 subscribers and even has a testimonial page where the cheaters can tell others about their experiences. In the article, the mistress said that the wives are the other women. She detailed how she was able to go out on dates with these husbands, have hot steamy sexual encounters and then send them home to their wives and children. This absolutely blew me away! I couldn't believe that our society had become so bold and brazen as to openly discuss and promote adulterous affairs. Something that has historically been kept secret is now something that people are proud to be a part of.

Having both of those things come up around the same time that I began contemplating writing this book only served as confirmation for me that I was on the right track.

In my quest to learn more about the role of a mistress, I began to ask men questions. I began to do research and I even browsed websites that were created by mistresses to learn what they did to steal another woman's husband. The more I researched, the more determined I became to learn what it would take to become the best mistress I could become. I became a student and began learning about some of the things the mistresses were doing in and out of the bedroom. During my research, I realized that they were doing things for the married men in their lives that had never crossed my mind to do for my own man. I was learning their playbook. Any coach will tell you that if you can get access to the opponents' playbook, you will always win the game. And while researching and talking to people, I began to get a clear picture of where wives are missing the boat. We wives are simply not making our men a priority! That is the bottom line.

I also began to realize that being my husband's mistress was the woman that I was always meant to be and that every wife has a duty to become her husband's mistress. If we all commit to doing our parts in our relationships and sowed positive seeds without an expectation of a return, just maybe we will get a return anyway. And I also thought that it would be fun to step into a role that most people frown upon but within the confines of marriage.

And while I am writing this book, I am still on my journey. I have not made a complete 360 because I have acted negatively for so long that it became a part of who I was. But I can say that now I see the errors of my ways and have made a commitment to portraying Christ in every interaction that I have with everyone I come in contact with.

My marriage has suffered a lot of blows. There is a lot of damage that has been done. There have been a lot of words that have been spoken that cannot be taken back. I have a lot of making up to do. Now I am on a journey of trying to define who I really am in the context of marriage and making sure that my definition lines up with the expectations that God has of me. But as long as I keep God's happiness ahead of my own, I have no doubt that I will be able to have a successful, mutually fulfilling relationship with my husband.

Chapter 1

Do I Really Have the Power to Change My Marriage?

"The man said, The woman you put here with me—she gave me some fruit from the tree, and I ate it."Genesis 3:12 (NIV)

Women have the power to influence men to become great leaders or simple followers. The influence of a woman can change the course of the world. Eve influenced Adam to disobey God and caused great turmoil between men and women that extends to modern times. Delilah influenced Sampson to tell her the secret to his strength, then she used it to turn him from God and to betray him.

Women have the power to influence a man, meaning we have the power to influence the world. Can you imagine Barack Obama without Michelle, or Bill Clinton without Hilary? What would Abraham have become without Sarah by his side? What about Jacob in the book of Genesis? Rachel influenced Jacob to give up 14 years of his life in order to have Rachel become his wife. What kind of men would these men have become without the influence of their women? The support, love, and encouragement of Michelle and Hilary took Barack and Bill all the way to the White House!

So, do you really have the power to change your

marriage? The answer to that question is YES!

Knowing that we possess such influence gives us a certain responsibility to do what we can to support, assist, and encourage the men in our lives to become all that God created them to become.

Our men need us. They need us to help them through the rough spots. They need us to comfort them when they struggle. They need us to go before God on their behalf, seeking mercy, grace, and favor.

Understand that God created you as sufficient. God created you to be enough. You already have everything inside of you to turn your marriage around and you have everything it takes to get the type of marriage that you have dreamed about since you were a little girl.

As a wife, you are the woman with the power and there is nothing that can stop you from finding fulfillment no matter what state your marriage is in. You are intriguing, strong, beautiful, powerful, sexy, smart, and courageous because that's how God made you. That's the way He made all women. You have no competition because no other woman can hold a candle to you when it comes to meeting the needs of your husband. You are the standard. Yes, that's you. You are the special woman in his life. A woman full of grace, confidence and strength that is capable of making great things happen is who you are. When it comes to love, sex and marriage, the sky is the limit for you. You are a woman full of drive and determination. You are the woman that holds it all together. You are a woman that deserves a great marriage. There is no limit to the power that you possess as a wife. Your husband may be driving the boat but you are the sail that keeps the ship moving in the right direction.

So my dear friend, please recognize that you are powerful beyond comprehension. You've just experienced some setbacks along the way that distracted you from being all that God created you to be.

But your husband didn't give a ring to anyone else. You were chosen! He knows what he has at home. He recognizes what a prize you are. You are the woman that completes him. That's why he is still around. He may complain about some of the things you do, but he hasn't gone anywhere. That fact alone speaks volumes to the value he has placed upon you as his wife. You are the caregiver, counselor and friend. You are the feminine, softer side of him. You are a mistress. You are the woman of his dreams. And you have the ability to help your husband become all that God dreamed for him.

He may not even believe his own value, worth, or abilities, but as his wife, it is your job to let him know that he is capable of doing great things and becoming a great man. By encouraging him, giving him unconditional love, and showing respect for him, you are healing the wounds of his past caused by the words of others and building his self esteem and confidence. When you begin telling him how capable he is and how much you believe in him, you will begin to see the transformations that you've been praying about. There is something about getting respect and the support of your woman that pushes a man to new heights. Neither Barack nor Bill would have had the confidence to seek out the position as President of the United States of America if they had Michelle or Hilary telling them they were unqualified and would never be successful. I imagine the exact opposite is true. These wives had to be their husbands' biggest supporters and loudest cheerleaders for both of these men to rise to such great heights.

And the same is true of all wives. We hold the keys that can unlock the destined paths for our husbands. The key of respect and the key of support will turn our husbands' hearts towards ours and hopefully towards the God in us. It will make them want to rise to the occasion to be the men we are telling them that they are capable of becoming.

So as a wife and a woman that has been given the power to influence your husband, don't just sit on the sidelines of your marriage. You have the power to help him fly to new heights. So why not use it? This is your opportunity to become the wife you always wanted to be.

Chapter 2

Who is the Mistress?

Being a mistress is a privilege and an honor which comes from holding the title "wife". But whenever a person hears the word mistress, there is almost always an automatic negative emotional and/or physiological response. Historically, the mistress is considered a home wrecker that is competing for another woman's husband. But recently, I ran across an alternative definition for the word Mistress. In the dictionary, a mistress is defined as [2] "a woman who has power, authority, or ownership as the female head of a household, a woman who employs or supervises servants, a woman who is in charge of an establishment, a woman of nobility having a status comparable to that of a master, a woman who has achieved mastery in some field". In fact, the traditional definition of a mistress, as a woman who has a relationship with a married man, ranked as number 7 out of 8 other examples that appeared on the list. My discovery of the real definition of a mistress opened my eyes and understanding of what God meant when he told me to become my husband's mistress. A mistress is not a home wrecker, she keeps the home fires burning. A mistress isn't evil, she is an entrepreneur. She isn't desperate, she is desired. A true mistress is a woman in full control and a force to be reckoned with. A mistress is someone's wife. A mistress is someone's mother. A mistress is the woman described in Proverbs 31.

The woman described in the bible in Proverbs 31, who I affectionately refer to as Mrs.31, is the type of woman that makes things happen. She doesn't have time for idleness or gossip because she is an entrepreneur who has goals, plans and aspirations. She is busy putting things into motion to ensure that her dreams come true and that they are of benefit to herself and her loved ones. Her man is not an afterthought or a chore on her to-do list. He is a priority for her and she is dedicated to helping him become the man that he was created and designed to become. Her man is envied by other men because this woman is well rounded, balanced, responsible, nurturing and fulfills her man in every way. She is a woman that can do it all and still make her man shine in the spotlight. She is a woman that other women admire, not only for her physical appearance, but also for her willingness to work with the talents that she has been given by God. She is a business woman who goes into the world with confidence in her abilities. Her money is in order, her household is in order, and she is able to have it all because she finds ways to market her skills to bring in extra money. She is not a woman that makes excuses about why she can't get things done. She is a woman with a plan. She is a woman who is organized. She is a woman in control.

So from this point forward, when we discuss becoming a mistress, we will be looking to our description of Mrs.31 for guidance. When you read the word mistress in this book, I want you to think about Mrs. 31 and the traditional definition of a mistress. I will use the word mistress to refer to both. I will use Mrs. 31 to give you a biblical reference and use the traditional definition of a mistress to give you a practical reference on how to interact with your husband.

Traditional Mistresses

Before we move further into the discussion about becoming your husband's mistress, let's look at two types of traditional mistresses: The Mistress of Opportunity and The Fantasy Mistress.

The Mistress of Opportunity is the woman your husband turns to when things are not going well in his relationship with you. The money isn't right. The kids are acting up. And you are always complaining about him. This is the woman he begins to talk to because he cannot share his true feelings with you. At first she is someone he can vent to. Then she becomes his counselor who gives him advice. Then she begins to share her story with him. Then he begins talking to her on the phone. Then he begins meeting her some place to talk more in depth about their personal problems. Now they are friends and confidants and are talking frequently. Then the conversation changes and is no longer about his challenges at home but about how he appreciates having someone who understands him and is easy to talk to. Then he begins to share his dreams and ideas with her. Then he begins wondering how more fulfilling his life would be if *she* was his woman. Then he gets more comfortable with her and begins expressing his fantasies about her. Then the affair begins.

The Fantasy Mistress is the woman who is arm candy. She is the fantasy that most men dream of. She is the type of woman that men pay for. She is attractive, skilled in/out of the bedroom and constantly feeds his ego. She is confident and isn't afraid of trying new things. She is adventurous and daring. She is the one your husband cannot get enough of. She makes him feel like he can rule the world and encourages him to dream big. She is the one whose bills will get paid even if the electricity is shut off at his own home. He would do anything to keep her interested.

There is nothing special or magical about the Mistress of Opportunity or the Fantasy Mistress. Neither of them are doing or saying anything that you are not capable of. They don't have a secret key to your husband's heart and aren't any wiser than you are. The only difference between you and them is the fact that they have made a personal investment in your husband's happiness and fulfillment. They don't have the burden of ensuring his clothes get picked up from the dry cleaners, caring for his children or cooking his meals. So they have nothing but time to think about and plan for spending time with your man to keep him engaged in their relationship.

All men have the need to have women that affirm them,

support them, listen to them and make them feel special. And they also desire a woman that has an adventurous side, keeps up her appearance and is a skilled lover. For those reasons, in your effort to become your husband's mistress, you must make it your mission to learn to be both types of mistresses.

Are you serious lady?

I know what you are thinking. Right now, you are thinking that trying to adapt yourself to be these types of women is just another thing on your already overflowing plate of responsibilities. Right now you are thinking "how I can possibly add anything else to the mix when I am already up to my eyeballs in things that I have to get done? Now I am being asked to invent this whole other woman who has all of these special capabilities? Yeah right, lady. Never gonna happen."

Then my counter point to you would be, how badly do you want your marriage to work? How far are you willing to go to ensure that the family you helped create, remains intact? What's it worth to you to keep your children from having to experience the pain of divorce?

You are no different than I am. You've already heard me mention my list of roles that I have to play. And that is the short list! And since I was already overworked and overwhelmed and couldn't imagine adding any additional things to my life, I simply had to re-prioritize my list of responsibilities because learning to become my husband's mistress was vitally important for the preservation of my family. For me, that meant that my children couldn't be enrolled in more than one activity at a time, I could not volunteer to teach anymore classes at church because it took too much time and energy to prepare for the classes, and I could only send out my daily devotional 2-3 days/wk instead of 5 days/wk. You see, everything extra that I was doing was stealing my time, energy and attention from the thing that mattered most-my family. I was constantly trying to encourage people, offer support and advice about a variety of topics but wasn't putting forth that same effort into the relationships that I had at home. Now just because I had to reprioritize my schedule and relinquish some of my activities doesn't mean that I will never allow myself to get back involved with doing those things. It just means that for the time being those activities needed to be put on hold until I straightened out my marriage and home life. Those activities aren't going anywhere. But my husband may if I don't get my priorities together.

So instead of dreading the idea of adding something else to your life, begin taking things away from your life. It won't mean that you are less of a Christian because you cannot continue to volunteer for every church event that comes along. You don't have to try to be supermom or win the mother of the year award by allowing your children to register for every sporting event the school offers. And you don't need to feel guilty for setting boundaries with others by adding the word "no" to your vocabulary. Because if you continue to offer your services to others at the expense of your marriage and family life, and lose everything you have in the process, then none of those activities would matter anyway. So one of the very first things to do on this journey towards becoming your husband's mistress is to re-prioritize your schedule with the goal of freeing yourself up physically, mentally, emotionally and spiritually.

On the following lines jot down some of the ways that you can free up more of your time and energy so you can make an investment in your marriage.

_____

_____

_____

_____

Be Realistic

It is completely unrealistic to think that becoming your husband's mistress is something that can be accomplished overnight. So don't get overwhelmed by thinking that you have to master every aspect of a mistress all at once. The problems in your marriage didn't occur overnight and won't be resolved overnight. So don't put that type of pressure on yourself. If you go into this with such high expectations of yourself it will soon begin to be less fun and feel more like work. And it will be less believable. This journey is not supposed to be a chore. So take baby steps. Don't go full blast no matter what state your marriage is in. The goal is to begin adopting habits of a mistress a little at a time.

The other thing I want to stress is that you shouldn't expect a return on your investment. Now don't let this statement discourage you from doing this vitally important work. If you are doing it with the expectation that you will get a return, then you will get easily frustrated and tempted to quit when your husband's actions test you. He may or may not believe you when you begin making changes for the sake of the relationship. He may be skeptical. Who wouldn't be? You are skeptical every time he says that he is going to change something about himself. So don't be surprised if his reaction is one of disbelief when you take on this new role. He may even resist your efforts at change or intentionally do things to test your authenticity. I am telling you now---Expect resistance. Expect to be sabotaged. Expect to be tested. But stay on course. Instead of looking for a return from your husband, do these things as a service to the Lord. The bible says that if you do it as a service to the Lord, then you will be rewarded (Ephesians 6:7-8). If you stay on course and determined not to be distracted, you will see positive changes in your relationship.

The Mindset of a Mistress

To the mistress, your man is the top priority in her life. To her, there is no other man in the world that can compare to him. And not only does she believe that, she operates from that belief system. He is never an afterthought. He doesn't come after the bills, the job, or a clean house. He is first place in her life. That is because she realizes that if she isn't meeting his needs, he can always go somewhere else to get those needs met. She is the ultimate aphrodisiac because she goes all out to please him. She keeps his attention with flattering words and by making him feel like he is the best lover she has ever had. She is open to trying new things and never rejects him. The mistress isn't a boring hag (at least not usually). A mistress is exciting, hangs on her man's every word, is passionate and adventurous. She makes time for him. She is excited to see him when he walks through the door. She is pleased to bring him dinner and the remote without complaining. She doesn't try to bully him into following her decisions or insult him because he thinks differently than she does. He is not made to feel less than a man with negative comments. Instead, she takes the opportunity to listen to his ideas and engage in discussions that shows him that his opinions matter to her. She sees his differences as unique, not as burdens. He is drawn to her because of her enthusiasm towards him. When she is with him he never feels like a failure. Sometimes he will walk away from everything in his life to continue to be able to experience the pleasure, validation and excitement she brings. She captures his attention, pleasures his body, strokes his ego and lures him with admiration.

This is the mindset of a mistress.

Who wouldn't be tempted by this type of woman? Everyone wants to feel admired, adequate and accepted. There is not a person walking this earth that wouldn't want the positive qualities that a mistress has to offer.

So the next thing I want you to do is to picture yourself in the role of the mistress. Put the book down and get a clear picture of yourself in this new role. I want you to imagine how you should act, imagine how you should talk and interact with your man, and imagine the traits that you should possess that draw your husband closer to you.

This is the mindset that you will need to adopt throughout this journey. Notice, I used the word adopt. Adopt means that this mindset will now become a part of who you are as a wife. We are not talking about trying this out and when things get better going back to your old ways of treating your husband. This mindset must become permanent in order for you to be successful. You cannot have the same mindset that you currently have and also have the mindset of a mistress. The two cannot co-exist. You must choose between them.

The Mistress is Powerful

I hope that what you have learned so far about the mistress is that she is powerful. She is not a second class citizen; she is not some mindless robot that has adopted a slave mentality just to stay in her relationship. She doesn't sacrifice who she is to please others or to convince others that she is worthy of their time and attention. She cannot be manipulated or coerced. She is not a weakling and is not controlling. No ma'am! The mistress is brilliant, wise, savvy and powerful. She uses her talents, skills and personality to get what she wants from her relationship. She uses subtle seduction in the form of support, respect, fun and sexual fulfillment to draw her man to her over and over again. She is the temptress. She is the woman that is desired and the woman he cannot get enough of. When he is with her he feels invincible. When he is with her he feels like he can conquer the world and make all of his dreams come true.

So becoming your husband's mistress doesn't mean relinquishing your power. Becoming his mistress means using your capabilities, power and influence as a woman to change the course of your relationship. It is in your power to have a great marriage. It is in your power to have a fulfilling sex life. It is in your power to create an environment in which your husband feels safe to love you the way you desire to be loved.

So when you read about the Proverbs 31 woman, don't be intimidated by how wonderful and perfect she seems. You are just as powerful, capable, intelligent and resourceful as she is. Mrs.31 wouldn't have been able to be so great if she lacked confidence in God or in herself. Therefore, your success begins with your own belief that you already have the qualities that makes you a great mistress. Dare to be bold. Dare to be unique. Stand out from the crowd and show others how a wife is supposed to treat her husband.

Chapter 3

The Work Begins

Now that we have a clear understanding of who the mistress is and how she operates, let's get to work implementing these changes in our lives.

Self Assessment

Before you can make the necessary changes in your relationship, you must first do a self assessment to get a clear picture of what areas you need to improve in. On the following assessment, rate yourself on a scale of 1-5 with 1 meaning "never/rarely", 3 meaning "sometimes" and 5 meaning "all of the time". It's important to be honest on this self-assessment. As Dr. Phil would say, "you cannot change what you will not acknowledge."

My husband is a top priority
I rate myself 1 2 3 4 5

I compare my husband to other men
I rate myself 1 2 3 4 5

I say negative comments to my husband
I rate myself 1 2 3 4 5

I go all out to please my husband
I rate myself 1 2 3 4 5

I make my husband feel like the best lover I've ever had
I rate myself 1 2 3 4 5

I am open to trying new things with my husband
I rate myself 1 2 3 4 5

I reject my husband
I rate myself 1 2 3 4 5

I am excited to see my husband when he comes home
My rating 1 2 3 4 5

I do things for my husband without complaining
My rating 1 2 3 4 5

I bully my husband into agreeing with me
My rating 1 2 3 4 5

I give my husband my undivided attention when he speaks
My rating 1 2 3 4 5

This self-assessment is not intended to make you feel
badly about your performance as a wife. It is only
intended to give you a picture of the areas that you are
excelling in and areas where you need improvements.
So don't beat yourself up just because you may not
have been the type of wife you dreamed of being. It's
okay if you haven't been perfect. None of us has. This
relationship has been rough. This relationship has tested
everything you thought you knew about yourself, God,
marriage and your husband. Who knew that this
relationship would be so draining, difficult and
discouraging? I haven't met many wives who can claim
many brownie points for making their husbands feel
like superman. But just because you may not have
treated your husband well in the past doesn't mean it's
too late. This is about adopting a new mindset and new

habits so you can begin to improve your marital relationship.

Every month you need to fill out a new rating scale on yourself to see what areas have improved. Then journal what changes you have seen in yourself, in your marriage, and in your husband since you began this journey.

Guiding Principles

There are 5 guiding principles that you must commit to in order to be successful on your journey towards becoming a mistress.

Principle 1: Be clear and honest about your motives.

The mistress is always clear about her motives. She may be in it for the money, the sex, the adventure or to find companionship without commitment. She never does things without a motive and she is always clear about that motive so she doesn't lose sight of why she is engaging in certain behaviors and activities.

Some of you may not want to change who you are. You may not think that changing who you are is the answer to enhancing and/or saving your relationship. That is ok. Just be honest with yourself. What is the REAL reason you want to begin this journey? What drove you to want to read this particular book at this particular time? Was your motivation to win the heart of your husband back, to save your dying marriage, to keep your husband happy at home, or to rekindle the spark in your relationship? Maybe you're doing it because you think having a failed marriage says something about you as a woman? Maybe you don't want to be embarrassed by admitting that your marriage is in shambles but you don't have a clue as to how to save it. Or maybe your motive is similar to mine; you are motivated by your own pursuit of happiness. Clarity and honesty are important because throughout the entire process, you will constantly need to remind yourself of your reason(s) for wanting to change how you think, how you behave and what you say all in an effort to change the course of your relationship. In essence, this book will challenge you to become a whole new woman. So if you don't know why you want to change, you will not be successful. Especially during the early stages when you begin implementing changes and encounter resistance or skepticism from your spouse. Also, if your motive isn't strong enough to give you the strength and determination you need to continue on this journey when you hit rough spots, then you need to re-examine your motive and possibly find a new one. Take a few moments to jot down the reason that you want to become your husband's mistress. If you write it down you can always reference it later if discouragement sets in.

Beginning this journey is important to me because:

_____

_____

_____

Principle 2: Operate in Love

The mistress often offers love and concern for her man to keep him interested. She may give him a bath, prepare all of his favorite meals and make him feel wanted and needed. And although she may not truly be in love with him, she offers him the illusion of love and he is willing to go to great lengths to keep her in his life.

You must commit to always operate from the framework of love. I understand that love is a risk. It's a risk because you never know what you're going to get. And when you have been hurt by love, you become unsure if you want to take that risk again. And the more times that you've given your love and been hurt, the less of a risk you are willing to take in the future. Whenever a woman has been hurt or disappointed by her spouse, often she begins looking at and interacting with him from a place of hurt and disappointment. The challenge is to begin looking at your husband with different eyes. The eyes are the window to the soul and if you look at him with anything other than love, he will know what is really in your heart.

Ladies, please hear me when I say this. Love and fear cannot occupy the same address. One will always try to overthrow the other and fight for control. And the result is a constant internal conflict-of wanting to give love freely but holding yourself back due to the fear of being hurt, rejected or disappointed. And since love and fear cannot live in the same space, in order to become your husband's mistress, you must choose love and reject the idea of fear. Fear has no place in this picture.

This is what God's word says about fear:

"Do not be afraid; you will not be put to shame. Do not fear disgrace; you will not be humiliated." Isaiah 54:4a (NIV)

"When I am afraid, I put my trust in you. In God, whose word I praise—in God I trust and am not afraid. What can mere mortals do to me?" Psalm 56:3-4 (NIV)

"So do not fear, for I am with you; do not be dismayed, for I am your God. I will strengthen you and help you; I will uphold you with my righteous right hand." Isaiah 41:10 (NIV)

"For I am the LORD your God who takes hold of your right hand and says to you, do not fear; I will help you." Isaiah 41:13 (NIV)

 You need to make the decision that you are going to love your husband and you are going to do it right. When you give him love, you need to love him in a big way, do it without expecting anything in return and love from the depths of your soul. You need to love him like you have nothing to lose.

But I am not referring to romantic love; I am speaking of God's type of love. This journey calls for agape love. Agape love is [3] "selfless, sacrificial, unconditional love". God's love gives. God's love is unconditional. And God's love is non judgmental. Agape love means loving the unlovable. It means loving the undeserving and the unworthy. It means loving people with all of their flaws, hang ups and bad habits. And it means accepting those that you don't find acceptable. God gives us agape love. Agape love does not mean turning a blind eye to the misdeeds or sins of others. It is not staying in a situation where you are being abused or degraded. But it is a gift that you freely offer to others.

"If I speak in the tongues of men or of angels, but do not have love, I am only a resounding gong or a clanging cymbal. If I have the gift of prophecy and can fathom all mysteries and all knowledge, and if I have a faith that can move mountains, but do not have love, I am nothing. If I give all I possess to the poor and give over my body to hardship that I may boast, but do not have love, I gain nothing". 1 Corinthians 13:1-3 (NIV)

The scripture clearly states that you can be a powerhouse in the church, have the ability to interpret and synthesize complex material, give up everything you have to help the poor and have enough spiritual power to move mountains but if you are lacking in love, you will gain absolutely nothing. Love was never meant to be held onto but to be expressed. We need to treat love like a gift that is better when given away. Look at the way God loves us. He doesn't keep his love to himself; he freely demonstrates his love each day that we breathe and have life. He gave us the ultimate gift of love when he sent Jesus to the cross on our behalf. So we don't need to be fearful of love or see love as a risky venture. Love is very powerful and the greatest gift you can give to anyone is non judgmental, unconditional love. When you choose to operate in non judgmental, unconditional love, that type of love has the ability to heal others, change their habits and free their hearts. No matter how things are between you and your husband, you can still love him as a person created in the image of God. In doing so, you will be blessed and will be a blessing to him.

On the following lines, identify why you have withheld agape love from your husband. Are you hurt or disappointed in him? Are you waiting for him to meet your needs first? Remember, be honest with yourself. You cannot become successful unless you are honest.

_____

_____

_____

Principle 3: Give Unconditional Respect

Men NEED Respect. Period. Without respect your man will never be the type of husband you desire.

The mistress would be a fool to ever disrespect her married lover. To do so would be counterproductive to what she is trying to accomplish by having him in her life. She shows him the ultimate respect and doesn't make him earn it by the things he does for her. She will show him respect regardless of how he is acting in an effort to keep him.

We will go into greater detail about unconditional respect later, but for now let's find out why you haven't given your husband the respect that he desires.

On the following lines, identify why you have withheld respect from your husband. Are you hurt? Disappointed in him? What has he done or not done to get your respect.

_____

_____

_____

Principle 4: Accept 1 Corinthians 11:9 (AMP) as pure, biblical truth. It says "Neither was man created on account of or for the benefit of woman, but woman on account of and for the benefit of man."

The mistress knows that she wouldn't be his mistress if she wasn't of benefit to him. If she was not meeting his needs for sex, companionship, fun, respect, etc she would have no place in his life. She always keeps that thought in mind when she interacts with her man because she knows that she can be easily replaced if she brings nothing to the table. Through her actions, words and deeds, she always shows him how she is a benefit to his life.

Accept it ladies. Don't try to fight it. Women were created for the benefit of the man. There is no use in trying to dismiss this scripture as old time religion. The word is clear and we don't have the authority to go against it no matter how much experience we have, how educated we are or how high our IQs are. God's word stands up against any challenge and will win every time.

So get used to it. Let this verse seep into your spirit. Repeat the verse daily or several times a day. These are words that you should strive to live by.

Identify your feelings and thoughts related to this verse when you first read it. Did you receive the message as truth?

_____
_____
_____

What resistance do you have concerning this verse?

_____
_____

Are you willing to accept this verse as truth? Why or Why not?

_____
_____

If you don't accept the verse as pure, biblical truth, how will that interfere with your ability to become your husband's mistress?

_____

Principle 5: Learn to adapt

The mistress adapts to her man's schedule and his preferences because she understands that his time is limited. She makes the most of their time together instead of fighting with him. She makes herself available at his request. She does the things he asks her to do to make him happy.

In order to become a successful mistress, a wife needs to learn to adapt to her husband. Adapting is defined as [4] "adjust to something, to become used to a new environment or different conditions". Yes, that's right ladies. With all of his flaws, hang-ups and bad habits, you must adapt yourself to him. Adapting doesn't mean approval. If your husband is doing wrong things or not following a godly lifestyle, adapting to him doesn't mean that you approve of his wrong doings. Adapting means to accept where he currently is in his life and not nagging or criticizing him concerning his lifestyle. Once you can accept where he is, then you begin praying and/or fasting that God changes his lifestyle. And while you are believing God for changes in his life, you continue to show your husband respect and honor as you have been called to do. If you can't adapt yourself because you simply don't want to or because you don't think your husband deserves it, then do it as a service to the Lord. Your husband may have done some things, said some things, or not done enough or said enough, but if you are his wife, then God expects you to adapt yourself to him (Ephesians 5:22) and show him respect. No excuses. If you want to be a wife that pleases God, then you must learn to adapt yourself to your husband.

What are some areas where you need to learn to adapt concerning your husband?

_____

_____

_____

These 5 principles should serve as a foundation for all of the work that you do. If you operate from these 5 guiding principles then you should be successful at becoming a desirable mistress for your husband.

But My Husband Doesn't Deserve All of This.

I know that you have been hurt. So have I. I know that you have been disappointed. So have I. I know that you envisioned something different for your marriage. So did I. You may not think that your husband deserves happiness. You may not believe that he deserves your best. You may feel that he is lucky that you have stuck around after dealing with all of his foolishness. I hear you. You are not alone in how you feel. For many years I have felt and spoken those exact words to my husband.

But the question that I have for all of you who are resistant to changing yourself is, how much is it costing you to stay in this painful situation?

I heard someone say that experience is the best teacher. And I agree. But I also believe that pain can be a powerful teacher as well. Pain forces you to face things that you'd rather deny. Pain makes you come out of your comfort zone and deal with a situation head on. Pain forces you to get rid of your preplanned goals and expectations and requires you to do something different. But pain also shows you just how much you can endure. So in my opinion, pain is one of the best teachers each of us can ever experience.

Is the pain of not having a fulfilling marriage enough of a motivator to get you to make the needed changes? You are already in pain. You have already been hurt. And you still stayed. So if you're going to stay married, instead of looking at him with disgust and disbelief, why not get the most from your relationship? Doing this work can't possibly cost you anymore than you have already given up just to be with him. At least if you transform yourself into his mistress, you can have a shot at marital satisfaction.

What I want you to know is that you can change the course of your relationship anytime you are ready. Even if you aren't convinced that he deserves to have you as a mistress, do it because you deserve to have a great marriage.

Chapter 4

Stripping 101

"Strip yourselves of your former nature [put off and discard your old unrenewed self] which characterized your previous manner of life" Ephesians 4:22a (AMP).

In addition to following the 5 guiding principles, becoming your husband's mistress will require you to go through a stripping process.

If you want to become a new person, you need to commit to doing a new thing and acting a new way. You need to strip yourself of maladaptive patterns and beliefs that keep your marriage from flourishing. You need to strip yourself of an attitude that doesn't serve your husband within the marriage. You may need to strip yourself of the beliefs you have regarding sex. And some of you may also need to strip yourself of your current wardrobe. In essence, you need to totally strip yourself of the parts of you that keep you from becoming the wife you were created to be and the wife that you desire to be.

There are two guarantees I can give you about the stripping process.

Number 1: It will not be fun.

Number 2: It will not be easy.

Stripping is a painful process that will require you to start over. The word strip is a verb so it is not something that can be done passively. It requires constant action. Think of stripping as peeling off all of the layers of yourself that no longer fit the vision that you have for your life. That is years worth of stuff that you will have to admit and expose about your behaviors and patterns. You must be willing to admit some things to yourself about yourself. So yes, you can expect to be uncomfortable.

Stripping will challenge you. Stripping will test you. Stripping will make you want to give up. But stripping is a necessary element for your spiritual growth and development and is crucial for the health of your relationship with your husband. You cannot continue on your current path of disrespecting, dishonoring and disregarding the man you call your husband. Learning to strip your mouth of negative words, your mind of negative thoughts and your heart of negative emotions is a requirement. You may also be required to strip yourself away from any person, place or thing that would keep you operating in the same negative way. Then you can strip for your husband whose heart will be turned towards you as you seek to become his mistress.

I want to take some time to do a little exercise with you to drive the importance of this stripping process home.

Let's take a look at two fictional resumes.

As we all know, the purpose of a resume is to allow someone to "sell" herself on paper to convince any potential employer that she is qualified and capable of doing a particular job. Generally speaking, a resume should include an objective, which states the person's goal and a list of past work experience.

As a side note, please don't ever send a resume that looks like this to any potential employer. As a person who has overseen the hiring of many employees over the past 12 years, trust me when I say that a resume like this will get tossed into the trash!

Resume #1

Objective (goal)

To use my executive level management experience to improve business outcomes.

Work Experience

Job Title: Nanny
Duties: Responsible for babysitting children ages 5-8, preparing meals, playing with kids.

Job Title: Event coordinator
Duties: plan children's birthday parties for a museum, order supplies, decorate space.

Job Title: Tutor
Duties: Tutor middle school aged students in math and science at local school.

The objective (goal) states that the applicant will use her executive level management experience to improve business outcomes. However, according to the person's work history, she has no experience as an executive level manager. All of her work experience indicates that she would be more suited for a job working with children. Therefore, it is safe to say that since she has no previous experience as an executive level manager, she is not likely to meet her stated objective (goal).

Now compare Resume #1 to the next resume.

Resume #2

Objective (goal)

To use my executive level management experience to improve business outcomes.

Work Experience

Job Title: Executive Account Manager
Duties: Responsible for managing a team of 12 account managers in a large investment firm.

Job Title: CEO
Duties: Manage the daily operations of a fortune 500 company.

Job Title: Chief Operations Manager
Duties: Manage 85 employees for a local hospital.

Job Title: President and Owner
Duties: Owned and operated a business employing 80 people.

As in the first example, the objective (goal) states that the applicant will use her executive level management experience to improve outcomes for business. Her work experience demonstrates that she has executive level management experience and presumably is knowledgeable of the management field. So based on this resume, the objective (goal) is clearly in line with the person's previous work experience. Not only does she desire to be a top manager but she also has the past experience to show that she can do the job. So her objective (goal) matches her experiences.

I use this example of a resume to illustrate why it is important to go through the stripping process. As a wife, if you say that your objective (goal) is to have a successful marriage but your previous experience of interacting with your husband doesn't line up with that objective, you will never achieve your objective (goal). You cannot possibly have a successful marriage when what you bring into your relationship is disrespect, dishonor and discouragement, etc. Therefore, you must strip yourself of your previous maladaptive patterns and create new experiences in order to reach your objective of having a successful marriage.

The Stripping Process

So what does stripping look like? Stripping is composed of 5 key elements.

Element #1: Submitting to God's ideas about

marriage

The first step in the stripping process is to submit to the beliefs about marriage that God has outlined in his word.

This is what the bible says about marriage:

a. "Therefore a man shall leave his father and mother and be joined to his wife, and they shall become one flesh. And they were both naked, the man and his wife, and were not ashamed" Genesis 2:24-25 (NKJV).

This means that the husband and wife are to be on the same team. You should both be fighting to achieve the same goal of having a successful marriage and family life. You shouldn't view your husband as your enemy. You are life partners and should have each other's back no matter what the circumstance or challenge. You and your husband should be totally transparent and unashamed to share your deepest fears, hurts and vulnerabilities with each other. There should be a level of comfort and trust between you that when you share information with each other both of you are assured that the information will remain confidential and won't be used against each other.

Additionally, when the scripture says that you are to be joined to each other, that means that there is not enough room in the relationship for more than 2 people. So stop inviting others in to have an opinion on your marital matters.

b."Submit to one another out of reverence for Christ. Wives, submit yourselves to your own husbands as you do to the Lord. For the husband is the head of the wife as Christ is the head of the church, his body, of which he is the Savior. Now as the church submits to Christ, so also wives should submit to their husbands in everything" Ephesians 5:21-24 (NIV).

Now, this may not be popular. It may go against your feminist beliefs. But since God created marriage, you need to look to Him to show you how to make your marriage a success. Both of you should be submissive and respectful towards each other. Wives must also learn to respect the hierarchy that God has established for the Christian family and not step out of line by attempting to circumvent their husbands' authority. Making decisions without your husband's approval and input is the reason you encounter so much resistance from him. He was created to lead his wife, not follow after her.

c. "And a woman who has a husband, who does not believe, if he is willing to live with her, let her not divorce him. For the unbelieving husband is sanctified by the wife, and the unbelieving wife is sanctified by the husband; otherwise your children would be unclean, but now they are holy" 1 Corinthians 7:13-14 (NKJV).

The only reason that your husband, if he is an unbeliever, has any chance of salvation is because you are his wife. That is because you are supposed to be an example of Christ in your husband's life. You are supposed to demonstrate love, forgiveness, compassion, kindness and mercy in an effort to win him over into God's family. So if the only reason that you want to leave your husband is because he doesn't follow Christ the same way you follow Christ, then you need to look to God to determine if you have just cause to leave him. It may be that you were put in his life to lead him to Christ. So if you give up, what will happen to him?

Element #2: Find and Seek Forgiveness

"And when you stand praying, if you hold anything against anyone, forgive them, so that your Father in heaven may forgive you your sins."Mark 11:22 (NIV)

Healing cannot take place until there is forgiveness. So the next thing you need to do is to ask for forgiveness. You need to ask your husband and God to forgive you for being critical, condescending, unfaithful, untrustworthy or any other negative thing that you have been in your marital relationship. You will not be able to move forward until you forgive your husband for not living up to your expectations. You will also need to forgive yourself for not being the type of wife that you are capable of being and for allowing your husband's actions to get you off track.

Element #3: Learn to capture your thoughts

It is vitally important that you begin changing your thoughts about your husband and about your marriage. The word of God gives instructions on exactly how to accomplish this. You are taught that in order to change your thoughts you must learn to take your negative thoughts captive.

"Casting down arguments and every high thing that exalts itself against the knowledge of God, bringing every thought into captivity to the obedience of Christ" 2 Corinthians 10:5 (NKJV).

What exactly does that mean? It means that all of your negative beliefs, ideas and attitudes regarding yourself, your relationship and your husband need to be deleted from your life. You must consciously cast down any belief or thought that does not line up with God's word. You must take your thoughts captive.

What are 3 things that we know about people in captivity?

1. They usually don't turn themselves in and have to be captured.

2. They must be led to the place where you want them to go.

3. They will always try to escape.

So when the word says bring your thoughts into captivity that simply means that you need to recognize that your negative thoughts will not identify themselves. They will not give you notice that they have entered into your mind so you must capture them when they show up. Next, you must lead those thoughts where you want them to go. You can no longer entertain negative thinking. You can't afford to have those negative thoughts roaming freely in your mind. But you are to bring them under the authority of Jesus Christ. Last, you must recognize that the negative thoughts will always try to escape and show up in your mind again. Just because you have been victorious at controlling your thoughts one day doesn't mean that the victory will last forever. Casting down negative thinking will be a life-long process.

Element #4: Put your blinders back on and begin meditating on your husband's positive traits

Along with capturing your negative thoughts, you also need to begin training your mind to think positively about your husband.

Despite disappointing and hurting you, you have chosen to stay in the relationship with him for a reason. So he must not be all bad all of the time. Your job is to identify his positive characteristics and allow your mind to stay focused on them. Do you like the way he interacts with the kids? Is he funny? Does he help with the chores? Does he keep your car washed and filled with gas? Does he keep the lawn mowed? Those good traits are where your thoughts should be every time an image of him pops into your head.

You have no problems ruminating over all of the things that he does wrong. Turn your focus on appreciating him for the things he does well.

A mistress chooses to keep her blinders on. She cannot afford to see her man as anything less than perfect. If she begins to focus her attention on how flawed he is, she will begin interacting with him in a different way. Consequently, she risks losing his interest which will jeopardize their relationship. And as his mistress you need to put your blinders back on.

Begin meditating on all of the things that you appreciate about him. When you first dated, you were giddy over the thought of your man. You replayed the jokes he told, the care he showed you and how he treated others and you allowed those thoughts to penetrate your mind all day long. If he did have a flaw, you quickly dismissed that thought. So you became excited to see this wonderful man every time he walked through your door. You told everyone how wonderful, thoughtful, handsome, and funny he was. You built up so much anticipation about this man to others that they couldn't wait to meet him. You treated him like he was God sent here to protect you, provide for you and to make you happy.

You must allow yourself to get carried away with good, positive thoughts about your man again. Learn to disregard those characteristics that are just plain annoying and that get underneath your skin. I know that it's upsetting that he won't clean up after himself after you have taken the time to put his items away. I know that he can test your patience because he doesn't lift a finger to help you around the house but has the nerve to complain because certain things aren't done to his liking. I get it! But for the sake of your sanity and your relationship, learn to stay focused on what he does right, instead of concentrating on what he does wrong.

Element #5: Begin speaking positive words over yourself, your husband and your relationship

The last thing you must do is to change your words. Your words need to line with the type of marriage you want and desire, not with the type of marriage that you currently have. It is no longer acceptable for you to sit with your girlfriends and talk badly about your husband. And it is no longer acceptable for you to listen to other women talk badly about their husbands. When your friends try to drag you into a husband bashing session, you need to remind them that their husbands are merely a reflection of the type of wife they have been. Because if they were using their God given influences to the best of their abilities they would be wise enough to know that they hold a lot of power and are capable of influencing their husbands to be better men.

Begin confessing God's word over your marriage. Use

your mouth to ask God for His help in turning your marriage around.

"From the fruit of their mouth a person's stomach is filled; with the harvest of their lips they are satisfied" Proverbs 18:20 (NIV).

In other words, you will have whatever you speak. Whatever you say, you will receive. So begin making positive confessions of faith. God cannot and will not bless you with a better marriage if you are constantly complaining about the blessings He has already given to you. You must prove that you are trustworthy to handle more than you currently have.

"Whoever can be trusted with very little can also be trusted with much" Luke 16:10a (NIV).

Examples of positive faith confessions....

Lord I thank you that my husband is your perfect provision for me.

Lord I thank you I am the wife that my husband desires.

Lord I thank you that my marriage is healed and experiencing positive changes and growth.

Whenever you find yourself reverting back to familiar habits and attitudes, you will be challenged to remind yourself that you are no longer a wife, but a mistress. When the temptation to criticize him rises up in your spirit, intentionally switch your attention on his positive qualities and continue to pray about any concerns you have about him. Now, there will be times that you may have slip ups but when that does happen, apologize quickly and sincerely and get back on track. You must immediately begin thinking about ways the mistress would interact and engage her man.

This stripping process will not come naturally. In fact, it will go against your very nature and at times seem overwhelming. But eventually, with consistency, those desires associated with your former self should disappear.

In every instance, stripping will require work, effort and action.

Chapter 5

The Mistress is Supportive

A mistress is supportive in a way that invigorates and inspires her husband to become a success in every area of his life. The ability to provide encouragement and emotional help are gifts God gave women to enable us to be able to speak to a man's deepest needs.

So in order to be a supportive mistress you must learn to be an encouraging wife.

The Importance of Encouragement

"But encourage one another daily, as long as it is called today" Hebrews 3:13a (NIV).

This is one of the most difficult scriptures that I have found in the Bible. It's not difficult because of what it is asking me to do; it's difficult because of how often it is telling me to do it. Between getting the kids ready for the day, going to work, cooking, cleaning, and paying bills, I rarely have the opportunity to just sit and relax or get a quiet moment to myself. So outside of sending my daily devotionals to a small group of women, encouraging others daily is not something that has been on my priority list.

But as I sit and think about why God would have included this scripture in his word, I began to realize the impact that encouraging someone would have on his or her life. God is not asking me to stand on the corner and encourage everyone who passes by. He isn't asking that I become a missionary and travel the world to lift someone's spirits. He is simply asking that I make a conscious effort to encourage someone I have contact with every day. And when I really think about it, He is not asking me to do any more than I want to do anyway. I live in a house with a husband and two children who would benefit greatly from an encouraging word.

Encouragement makes people feel adequate just as they are. Encouragement helps someone find a bright spot in a gloomy day. Encouragement will help people face their fears and soar to new heights. Encouragement simply means [5] "giving hope or support to someone." When people are encouraged by someone that matters to them, they have a tendency to flourish. So I have learned that it is crucial that I adopt the habit of speaking a word of encouragement to my husband on a daily basis.

This is also something that every other wife should begin doing. Each of us needs to offer our husbands the same type of support that we would offer a girlfriend that is struggling in some area. Women tend to have more compassion for their girlfriends than for their husbands. Why is it that we have more patience and compassion for our friends regarding their various issues (even after we have told them what they should do on at least 5 different occasions) but don't extend that same patience and compassion to our life partners? We don't end our friendships because our friends don't follow our advice, so why are we so quick to end our relationships when our husbands don't do what we want them to do?

As a mistress, your challenge is to find an area where your husband needs to be encouraged and begin offering encouragement to him on a regular basis. Has he experienced discouragement because he is not where he would like to be in life? Or maybe he just needs to hear kind words because no one has ever spoken any into his life. Encourage him so that he never feels inadequate. Encourage him so that he never feels like a failure. Encourage him when he feels like he has been called by God to do something different in his life. And when your husband faces difficult situations, be there to encourage him to seek God. Allow God to use you to be a strong support system to your husband. There is no one that is more qualified than you to do the job. And when you begin offering him encouragement, resist the urge to tell him what you think he should do unless he asks you. Just be there to listen to him vent or express frustration.

Offering Comfort

Being supportive also means providing comfort to your husband. An important way that you can comfort him is by having sex with him.

"Then David comforted his wife Bathsheba, and he went to her and made love to her." (2 Samuel 12:24 NIV).

I know this may sound strange to some of you but sex can be comforting to both males and females during periods when stress levels are high. That is because during sex, endorphins (the "feel good" –hormone) and Oxytocin (the "love and attachment" hormone) are released.

[6]"Stress and pain are the two most common factors leading to the release of endorphins. With high endorphin levels, we feel less pain and fewer negative effects of stress." Endorphins interact with the opiate receptors in the brain to reduce our perception of pain and act similarly to drugs such as morphine and codeine. In addition to decreased feelings of pain, secretion of endorphins leads to feelings of euphoria."

[7]"In humans, Oxytocin is thought to be released during hugging, touching, and orgasm in both sexes. It is known to play an active role in the formation of relationships, bonding and building trust between people." For those reasons Oxytocin has been commonly referred to as the "love and attachment" hormone.

Now hopefully you understand why your husband can be stressed to the max or in great emotional distress and still want to have sex with you. Sex is a great stress reliever which provides comfort and feelings of euphoria. Your husband is comforted by having your arms and legs wrapped around him as you embrace him during love making. So don't neglect offering him comfort in this way.

The Helpmeet

"And the LORD God said, It is not good that the man should be alone; I will make a help meet for him" Genesis 2:18 (KJV).

Loosely defined, a helpmeet is a woman that helps meet the needs of her husband and family. Other biblical definitions of a helpmeet are "wives that are suitable, adaptable, satisfactory and complementary of her husband." (AMP)

God created women to be an integral part in the spiritual development of men to help them reach their full potential as leaders of the home and community. The helpmeet was created to come along beside their husbands to offer assistance in advancing God's agenda. So being a helpmeet means that you must be willing to do whatever you can to assist your husband with finding and achieving the goals that has been set by God for your family.

As a helpmeet you are expected to be of service to your husband. It doesn't mean becoming his mother, his maid or his servant. It just means being of service. In other words, having the mentality that you will do whatever is needed in order to help him rise to a place of leadership in your home. That may mean that you ensure the household is in order, the finances are on point or that you allow him to be the primary decision maker. It may also mean that you help build his confidence in his ability to become a success in life. Wherever your heart and the word of God leads you concerning being of service to your husband is your job as his help meet.

When you begin to operate from the framework of being a helper to your husband, then and only then will he become the husband you want and father to your children that you prayed for.

The Helpmeet Works

Proverbs 31:21 says that Mrs. 31 "didn't fear the snow for her family because all her household are doubly clothed in scarlet." That simply means that she wasn't worried about how her family's financial needs would be met because she made preparation in advance.

Mrs. 31 was a working wife. This wife was a business woman. This wife was creative. This wife was a force to be reckoned with. She was a woman that made positive things happen for herself and for her family. She was not sitting at home watching soap operas or gossiping with her girlfriends while her husband was in the city working. She wasn't waiting for her husband to come home with his biweekly paycheck. This wife was an entrepreneur whose day began before her husband's did. The scripture says that she was gathering wool and working with her hands to develop it. She was into real estate. She helped the poor. She sewed and sold her garments. This mistress used her talents and God given skills to earn a living.

In today's day and time it is often necessary for the wife to have a job outside of the home to help supplement her husband's income. Unless the husband is making a six figure income or unless the family is living very modestly then a wife may have to work to help meet the needs of her family. But there are women in this world that will watch their husbands struggle financially and do nothing to help them. Although a man has the ultimate responsibility of taking care of his family, in an era where gas, food, and utility prices are always changing, often a man needs help in the area of finances. And for a wife to refuse to help alleviate this extra stress is not biblical and is almost a guarantee that her marital relationship will crumble.

It is great that you want to pursue your education or to stay at home with the kids but if doing so comes at the expense of your family's financial well being and security then those things are not beneficial. It is not beneficial for your relationship if your husband is bringing home an income that barely meets the needs of the family while you do nothing to help generate extra cash. Refusing to help is selfish, no matter how great your reasons are.

A lot of women, including myself, have this desire to

spend time raising the kids or doing meaningful work rather than just having any kind of job. For those of you who may feel this way, I know what you are going through. Although I have 2 degrees, some certifications and specialized skill sets, I have not wanted to work for years. It stemmed from having to work while raising a child on my own, working a full time job, going to school part time, doing a 20 hour a week internship all at the same time for four consecutive years. My days were between 15 and 18 hours long. I was physically, mentally, emotionally and spiritually drained all of the time while trying to place myself in a better position to adequately care for my child. So when I got married, one month before completing my masters program and internship, I was tired of working. I needed a break and wanted to rest and felt that my husband could take care of his new family all on his own. So I proceeded to inform my husband of my desires and presented a "carefully" thought out plan to him on how we could make it work with only his income. I really thought it was a good plan and that it would work beautifully. That is, until my husband pointed out one very important detail that never entered my mind. He affirmed that my plan would work with only his income supporting the family as long as we agreed that we would not want any more than we already had in life. As long as we were satisfied with our current home and never planned to move; as long as we were satisfied with our cars and never planned to upgrade and as long as we were satisfied with not going on vacation, shopping or participating in recreational activities as often as we wanted, we would be fine financially. Once my husband was able to bring me back to the reality of what I was proposing, the decision was an easy one to make. If I wanted to build a comfortable life with my husband without the stress of worrying about our ability to afford certain things, I knew I needed to keep working to keep us moving in the same direction that we had planned prior to the wedding. Me not working came with sacrifices that neither my husband nor I were willing to make.

But the desire of not wanting to work never left me. So I went from job to job hoping that each one would make the necessity of work more bearable. I had a new job almost once a year. I switched jobs so often that it became a running joke among my family and friends as they tried to keep up with where I was working from month to month.

I worked, and when I had energy left, I would write. I was trying to promote my first book, secure speaking engagements, send daily devotionals, keep my webpage current, be a good wife and mother, etc, not to mention battling fatigue from a chronic illness and getting back injections from a car accident that kept me in bed for 2-3 days at a time. I didn't possibly know how to continue with my current load of responsibilities and be a good mother. So another reason I didn't want to work was so I could spend more time raising my children.

I know what it is like to be at a job when your heart is longing to be a mother to your children. I can't tell you how many days my heart broke because my children were spending more time with the babysitter than with me. It got so bad at one point that my eldest son Jonathan began calling my babysitter mommy. And when I had a second child, I really began to question if working was the right thing for me and my children. Like his older brother, when my youngest son Jason turned 3 he would wake up in the morning happy to see me and then get sad because I had to drop him off at daycare instead of staying at home with him. I had experiences with both children crying and pleading with me to stay home with them instead of going to work. I felt torn. I had a financial obligation to them but I also had an obligation to raise and nurture my babies.

I wasn't a bad or neglectful mother and spent as much time with my kids each day as I could. But after driving 1.5 hours to work, working all day and driving up to 2 hours back home, there was only about 1.5 hours a day that I had to spend with my kids before it was time for them to go to bed. I was trying to be superwoman but no human could keep up with those types of demands without some area suffering. And the area that was suffering most was my ability to be everything I desired to be for my children. And this cycle went on and on until it became unbearable.

My spirit began demanding that I be true to what it was guiding me to do which was to be available for my kids. I was reminded by God that until I followed the path my spirit was leading me down, I would never have peace and contentment. I would forever be chasing a dollar and lose precious moments that I could never get back with my two boys. So when my youngest son turned 4 and my oldest son entered the 7th grade, I decided it was time to stay home.

Now I just had to get my husband on board with the new plan.

Let me give you a little history on us. For the entire length of our relationship, including the dating phase, my husband made it very clear to me that he did not want a stay at home wife. Both of his parents worked and he felt very strongly that he and his wife should always work. So to approach him with my idea of quitting my job was not something that I looked forward to doing. I had quit my job 3 years earlier when God told me to leave that particular job but my husband didn't have a vote in that decision. Consequently, he was resentful during that time when I was not working. I was doing contract work as a therapist and secured a book deal for my first book *God's Girl: A Daily Word to Encourage Women to Live Out Their Purpose* but I didn't have a full time job and no full time pay. Eventually, out of necessity, I had to return to the workforce.

But this time, almost 4 years later, was different. My husband and I were in a much better place in all aspects of our marriage and he would have a full vote in the decision this time around.

So I began sharing my heart's desire with him. I also began praying and sowing financial seeds that his heart would be in favor of what my spirit was leading me to do. I kept praying that God would speak to my husband's heart because there was no way I was going to stop working without his blessing. And while I waited for God to answer my prayers, I was careful to maintain all of my financial obligations to my family and the church.

Then one day it happened. I cannot remember the details of what we were discussing but I remember it was at the end of a disagreement. My husband gave me permission to stop working to pursue what God was calling me to do. Nothing had changed about his disinterest in having a stay at home wife but he didn't want to be the reason why I didn't follow my life's path. So he conceded. He didn't seem happy or unhappy, just neutral. Not at all what I was expecting. I pictured in my mind that my husband would have this great epiphany from God and would come to me pleading for me to do the work of God. But since that didn't happen, I began to question if this was really the answer to my prayers.

I concluded that my husband was just going along with my idea in order to keep the peace and to keep me happy. But secretly, I thought, he was resentful. So I continued reporting to work. After all we were just getting to a good place in our marriage and I didn't want to rock the boat. And while continuing to work, resentment towards my husband began to set in. I began to wonder if I would ever have what I desired in life if I remained in this marriage. On one occasion I actually said what I was thinking directly to my husband and his response surprised me. He became angry with me and was completely blown away by the fact that I was beginning to resent him after he told me that I could quit my job to fulfill my desire to spend more time at home. I responded by telling him that it was his lack of enthusiasm that made me question his sincerity. My husband explained that his enthusiasm would never match mine because it wasn't his dream, the dream belonged to me. He went on to explain that he didn't want to be blamed if there were financial struggles since we were used to living on two incomes. He expressed his worries about health insurance and the ability to enjoy life on a fixed income. And although he had concerns, he still wanted me to follow my spirit. So after many more discussions and battling my own internal fears, the day came when I turned in my resignation. And because of that decision, I was able to complete this book.

I shared my story with you to show you that I understand the struggle you may be facing about home and work life. I get it, ladies. But let me say this. You are expected to help your husband meet the needs of your family. And if that means that you have to get into the workforce to do so, then that is what you must be willing to do. That doesn't mean you will have to work the rest of your life, but you may depending on your personal financial situation. Don't put all of the pressure on your husband's shoulders to provide for your family. As Mrs. 31 demonstrates, a mistress is a woman that brings something to the table. By not doing so, you are setting your marriage up for resentment, discord and failure. Since you were created to be his helpmeet, until you step into the role of a working helpmeet, you will not experience true marital fulfillment.

If you don't want a traditional job, work for yourself. What can you do to ensure that the financial needs of your household are met? Find alternate ways to generate income if your husband is in agreement. Like Mrs. 31, find multiple streams of income. Stop giving your services and skills away for free. Ask yourself, what you can do to make money. Can you bake? That's how Mrs. Field got her start. Can you write? Can you do great decorations or plan fabulous events? Find ways to capitalize on your skills and talents to make a profit. Do whatever is profitable and gives you and your husband peace.

Or if you are like me, struggling between working and being at home, maybe it's time to step out of your comfort zone to explore your passions. Maybe it's time to downgrade your fulltime job to a part time job. Whatever changes you need to make, make them. But don't stop contributing to your household financially. You must make a financial contribution if your husband is not in a financial position to carry the entire load on his own.

Each marriage is different and couples will have to decide what works best for their marriage and the future plans of their family. Just as my husband and I had to decide together and agree on a plan, each wife must also make a joint decision with her husband regarding her employment status. You cannot be a mistress if you are worried about how the bills will get paid.

Affirmation

In addition to making a financial contribution, this new journey will require you to begin treating your husband as if he is already the husband of your dreams. A mistress doesn't waste time trying to mold her man, shape him, or manipulate him into becoming the man she wants him to be. She treats him as if he is the man that she's always dreamed of, her knight in shining armor. That's why he is willing to go to great lengths for her and to give her what she wants. She treats him as if he is adequate enough and as if he is more than she could have ever dreamed of for herself. When your man is being made to feel adequate and special it builds his confidence and self esteem and makes him want to do more for you.

"She comforts, encourages, and does him only good as long as there is life within her" Proverbs 31:12.

Do you see that ladies? As long as there is life in Mrs.31 she uses her life to encourage her husband and support him. Not until things get rough, or until he loses his job, or until he makes a huge mistake. But as long as she continues to draw breath from the living God.

So begin affirming your faith in your husband. Affirm to him that you made a good choice by marrying him. Affirm for him that he is acceptable just the way God made him. Affirm to him that he is enough to meet your needs. Begin using your mouth to build him up in private, in front of the children and in front of others. The more he hears kind, affirming words, the more respected and important he will feel. The more you hear the kind, affirming words that you are saying to him, the more positive you will begin to feel about him. Saying it aloud gives you the opportunity to hear positive things spoken about your mate which will eventually alter your perception of him. It will make you begin looking for things about him that validate your new perception of him. And this should enhance your relationship.

And when you begin affirming your husband, whatever words you use towards him must be based in fact. They also must be authentic and come from the heart. Don't tell him that he is a hard worker if he has never worked a day in his life. If you don't believe the words coming from your mouth, neither will he. You may not have a long list of good things to say about him. You may only be able to come up with one or two things. That's okay. Begin there. Don't force anything. As you begin looking at him from a new perspective, you will be able to add to this list of things to affirm him about. The goal is to be intentional and consistent.

It may be difficult for some of you to say anything positive to or about your husband because of past hurts. So for those of you who may be struggling to come up with anything positive to say about your husband, I will help you out:

1. Because of the blessing of being his wife, your husband has given you the opportunity to be a mother.

2. Your relationship with your husband has shown you how to be a confidant and a companion.

3. Being married to him has taught you how strong and resilient you are.

4. As his wife you have learned how to minister and support someone and your marriage has taught you life lessons that couldn't have been learned any other way.

5. Being married to your husband has strengthened your relationship with God because God is often who you call to deal with the issues in your marriage.

Yes friend, your husband has been a tremendous blessing to you. So let him know it. The bible says to give "honor to whom honor is due" (Romans 13:7).

Once you begin seeing your husband as a blessing from God, your list of affirmations about him will get longer and your affection towards him should begin to improve.

Admiration

Admiration is another form of support. To admire someone means [8] "to regard with pleasure, wonder, and approval; to have a high opinion of; esteem or respect."

The way to a man's heart is not through his stomach as we have been taught. The way to a man's heart comes from the admiration and respect that he gets from those closest to him- especially the admiration from his wife.

In The Lady, Her lover and Her Lord, Bishop T.D. Jakes points out this fact very clearly. In the book he says that men respond to praise in the same way God responds to praise. Praise and admiration moves the heart of a man.

But I have found that most of the time women bring preconceived ideas of marriage into their relationships and fight with their husbands to get them to conform to the image of marriage that we have in our minds so we can get our fairy tale ending. We erroneously believe that if we can just get them to act a certain way, believe a certain way and do everything our way, they will become the men we have always dreamed of marrying. Then we become angry, resentful and indignant when our husbands resist our efforts in converting them into our own personal prince charming.

Consequently, instead of offering praise and admiration to our husbands, many wives offer criticism and complaints. I heard Bishop Jakes say that "the spirit of criticism will often use scripture to give itself a reason to exist." Isn't that true ladies? We often throw out scriptures like Ephesians 5:25 which says "Husbands, love your wives, just as Christ loved the church and gave himself up for her." We will use this scripture to criticize our husbands for not loving us in a way we find acceptable. We think that our criticism will inspire change not realizing that criticism usually inspires rebellion. And every time we criticize them, it sends a message to them that tells them that they are not good enough for us.

Let me say this to all of the wives out there. It is a lesson that I have had to learn on my own through trial and many errors. If you married your husband thinking you could change him into the man you really wanted, that is the reason why you are so unhappy and discontent. If all of your efforts are centered on changing him as a person, then you have the wrong attitude and will continue to be dissatisfied in your marriage. Your focus should not be on changing who he is. You are not God. You cannot change the character or habits of another person. His last woman thought she could change him too. And so did every other woman who has had a serious relationship with your husband. Yet, he continues to do the same things and act the same way. That is because he is an individual with an individual personality, an individual set of beliefs, and a different upbringing. To change him means you would change him as the person that God created. And no woman has the right to ask anyone to become someone different in order to be in a relationship with her.

How can a woman of God stand and worship God but despise and complain about what God has created? How dare you tell him that he is unacceptable simply because he doesn't do things in the manner you deem acceptable. Your husband's differences are not a liability to your relationship, they are an asset. But women often see their husbands' differences as flaws that need to be corrected instead of assets that should be celebrated. His differences are what make him beautiful and unique and are to be celebrated, not criticized. Just as you, as a strong, vibrant, intelligent woman are beautiful because of your uniqueness, the same is true of your husband. So instead of criticizing, critiquing and trying to change him, learn to celebrate the many ways that he is different from you. Celebrate the many areas that you complete each other. He may be level headed when you are emotional, he may be strong in areas where you are weak and he may bring calm to a turbulent situation. Learn to celebrate and appreciate his differences. The fact that he is different from you is what makes you necessary in his life and vice versa.

Show Reverence

I once heard a speaker at a marriage conference say "if you and your husband were just alike, one of you would be unnecessary". And that is absolutely true! He was never created to be exactly like you. If so, God would have created him female. As long as you bring a different set of skills, perceptions and ideas to the table, you will always be an integral part of his life.

"And let the wife see that she respects and reverences her husband [that she notices him, regards him, honors him, prefers him, venerates, and esteems him; and that she defers to him, praises him, and loves and admires him exceedingly]" Ephesians 5:33b (AMP).

As the scripture encourages, go above and beyond in your admiration of your husband. That means that regardless of the type of mate your husband is, you should find something to give him admiration over. Men seek validation. They need to know that someone believes in them and think they are doing a good job. Admiring him will make him feel adequate, worthy and strong. He will never get tired of hearing how great he is. Affirming, admiring words are like kryptonite to a man which weakens him to the person who has offered them to him. That is the reason why he can be so easily enticed by another woman.

Force yourself to look beyond the hurts, disappointments and mistakes that your husband has made in your relationship. Look at him like he is the man of your dreams. Look at him with love in your eyes. Look at him as God's perfect provision for you. Once you take your eyes off of all of the areas you see as flaws and begin to enjoy him for who God created him to be, you will be able to get the marital satisfaction that you fought so long and hard to achieve.

Begin treating him as if the changes that you are

praying about have already taken place in his life.

When you take the time to tell your man all of the many ways that you admire how hard he works and how great he is, this will inspire him to want to do things that please you.

Breathing moment

I realize that I am throwing a lot of expectations your way. I know that you feel like you are being asked to do too much too soon. This is not easy work ladies. I warned you that you would be challenged and if I'm right, you are beginning to feel the pressure. I have been there. In fact, I am still there at times. That is why I asked you to pace yourself. You have way too many things on your plate to be able to implement all of these changes at once. Take it slowly. Take it one day at a time. And continue to breathe. Continue breathing until you can feel your blood pressure return to normal. This may be a good time to set the book aside and just digest everything you have learned so far and try to make sense of it all.

Chapter 6

The Mistress is Drama Free

[9]"Most men have affairs because of communication problems in their marriage or an empty gap that has grown in their marriage and they are unsure on how to approach it. They long for good happy company again without complications, and an affair is a good escape for them"

Chances are, if your husband had a girlfriend outside of his marital relationship, the woman he would choose would not be full of drama. Ideally, she would cause less drama in his life, not more or the same of what he gets at home. She would be easy to talk to and her home would be a place where he could relax and unwind. So in your effort to become your man's mistress, you need to learn to distance yourself from drama.

You know what I mean by drama. Crying because he doesn't let you have your way; being upset and angry because he wants to do something without you and the kids; withholding affection because you disagree with something he said. You know what I mean- DRAMA. DRAMA stands for Draining Reactions in an Attempt to Manipulate the Actions of others and is rooted in manipulation. You want your husband to act a certain way or make a certain decision so you behave like a 2 year old until he gives in. Oh you may not fall to the floor pounding the pavement with your feet while kicking your legs all over the place but you may let your tears flow uncontrollably as you attempt to make him feel guilty. Then you may accuse him of not truly loving you; because if he truly loved you, he would agree to do what you want him to do. That is DRAMA! And DRAMA is the furthest thing from a mistress's mind. A mistress recognizes that she must not do anything to cause her man to lose interest in her. She may be kicking and screaming on the inside but she will never show it on the outside.

Also, when you talk to your husband try to keep your emotions in check. We women, as adults, should be able to have a conversation without the crying and nose blowing. Every conversation doesn't call for tears so stop making it more dramatic than it needs to be. That doesn't mean that you can never cry, vent, or voice fears but that means that you don't cry, vent or voice fears to try to get him to do something differently. So if you are prone to crying, go ahead and cry about the issue prior to talking to your husband because drama is a complete turn off.

And speaking of crying, ladies please stop crying just because you feel like crying. If you need to cry for no reason, then do it alone in the bathroom or take a walk while you cry. We often bait our husbands in by crying so long and/or so loudly in an effort to get their attention and when they come to us to see what is wrong, we continue to cry while saying "nothing". Then after about 30 minutes, we will finally begin discussing what is on our minds. Say it with me ladies-

D.R.A.M.A. If nothing is wrong, then stop crying. If something is wrong, then be a big girl and use your words to express what is bothering you.

Men aren't mind readers. As much as we like to think that our husbands should know how we feel, what we think and how we want them to respond, most men have no clue from day to day what their wives are thinking. But we continue to attribute this supernatural ability to our husbands, and then become upset when they misinterpret us.

Save all of that drama for your conversations with your friends. Cry, throw your hands around, fall out on the floor when you are with your friends, not with your man. Because that type of behavior has no place in marriage. Save your very best for your husband. He should feel at ease when talking to you. He shouldn't be uncomfortable bringing up any issues, no matter how complicated, for the both of you to discuss. You can't get upset every time he brings up a difficult subject-even when it's about you. You can't get mad every time he asks you to change something about your attitude, your appearance or a bad habit. You have to be open to discussing and negotiating different things so both of you can be satisfied in the relationship.

Drama is Draining

You need to recognize that drama drains people and causes them to lose the desire to keep company with you. Any anything that drains your man's energy will not get the best that he has to offer. You don't want your husband to feel like being married to you is a job. He works all day long trying to provide for his family. He doesn't need to come home to your list of demands and complaints. He wants a wife that keeps his life easy and drama free. He wants a woman who knows how to talk about issues without bringing extra negative energy into the conversation. Remember, you don't want your husband to have a negative image of you in his mind. If he thinks he will come home to miss drama queen, he will be tempted to stay away from home just to get some peace. Listen to what this husband had to say:

I hate that my wife complains about everything. She always sees the cup half empty and has a pessimistic view about everything. I wish she would stop being so negative and bringing up issues all of the time. I want her to talk to me in a rational way, not with all of the crying, complaining, and negativity. Nothing seems to please her and she doesn't have a problem letting me know what I am doing wrong that makes her life miserable. I love my wife but she drains me with all of the drama she brings into the relationship. Nothing is ever easy in this relationship.

Stop playing games

There is a saying in the world that says that love is a game. If you are one of those people that subscribe to this mentality, then you have wrong thinking. Love is not a game that anyone should play but a gift that should be freely expressed and offered unconditionally. You are playing the game of love when you withhold sex and/or intimacy from your husband until he gives into your demands. And you are playing the game of love when you give him the silent treatment for not doing what you expected him to do. It's like playing a game of chess, placing your pieces strategically to ensure that you win. But that is not the bible's definition of love and that's why you never truly get your needs met in the relationship.

Let's look to see what the bible has to say about love.

"Love is patient, love is kind. It does not envy, it does not boast, it is not proud. It does not dishonor others, it is not self-seeking, it is not easily angered, it keeps no record of wrongs. Love does not delight in evil but rejoices with the truth. It always protects, always trusts, always hopes, always perseveres. Love never fails". 1 Corinthians 13: 1-.8a (NIV)

You don't have to play games to get your husband to change when you have God on your side. Games are for children, not for married women who want a strong, committed relationship. God doesn't have to manipulate us to love him and we don't have to manipulate others to get them to love us. There is absolutely no benefit in participating in game play because you will always end up a loser. That's because any changes that your husband makes won't be from the heart and won't last long. He is only making the changes so he can get back on your good side. So instead of playing games, you should be spending time at the feet of Jesus seeking assistance to get your husband to change his ways.

Stop playing with love as if it is a game because it is something that God takes very seriously.

K.I.S.S.

K.I.S.S. is an acronym that stands for [10] "Keep It Short and Simple".

Ladies, men don't want to have long conversations with us. They don't have the need to connect with us or work through problems by engaging in long discussions about the issues in the relationship. Most men are bottom line type of guys. All they want to know is the bottom line. They don't want to hear a history lesson on how the relationship got to this point. They don't want to know about other couples that are going through the same issues. They don't care about what your friends have to say about fixing the problem. They are simply interested in knowing what is wrong and coming up with a solution so they don't have to talk about it again. So while we are rambling on about how we arrived at this stage in our relationships, our husbands' insides are screaming "please get to the point!"

So for the sake of your man's sanity, keep your

conversations as short, simple and to the point as possible.

If you are a long winded person you may need to practice your conversation prior to approaching your husband. Or you may need to make an outline prior to talking to him to keep you from veering off track. This may sound excessive but in an effort to keep from annoying your husband and losing his interest, this may be a necessary step you need to take to prepare for a serious discussion. And as much as possible, refrain from giving a lot of background information and stay focused on the current issues and information related to those issues.

If you keep approaching him with lengthy conversations, eventually he will begin avoiding all conversations with you so he doesn't run the risk of having those "can we talk" moments.

Chapter 7

The Mistress is Respectful

Let me warn you now. This section on respect is quite long and that is intentional. The reason that we will spend so much time looking at this concept of respect is because without respect you will NEVER have a fulfilling marriage. Respect is as important to your husband as taking his next breath and if we wives don't figure that out soon, our marriages will be doomed to fail. So whenever you feel like you are ready, hold your breath and dive in head first.

Wives are often rude and disrespectful but then demand respect from their husbands. They place all of the expectations and rules on their men but refuse to accept the same. The reason I know this is because I was that type of wife.

Rules didn't apply to me. Especially after I had to forgive, put up with bad habits, clean up after and shouldered the majority of the responsibility of the household. I could not be told what to do and only considered doing what was asked of me if it was presented to me in the right way. I made the rules and held my husband accountable if they were broken. I made the majority of the decisions and always did what I wanted.

There were some days that I wouldn't have wanted to be married to me. My husband would never know what mood I would be in, what demands I would make, what issue I wanted to blame him for, etc. So he was constantly walking on egg shells around me just to keep the peace. And although I felt bad for the way I would act with him, pride would not allow me to cut my nonsense short in order to establish peace. So I stayed mad for as long as I wanted, stayed disrespectful for as long as I wanted and disregarded his thoughts, feelings and desires until I felt like being cooperative.

Now I want to be clear. I am not married to a weakling of a man who is incompetent, incapable or a pushover. He has always been in leadership roles with the companies that he has worked for and fully capable of making sound decisions. But if you are the youngest child growing up, you have developed various techniques and strategies for getting what you want the way you want it.

So whenever my husband tried to make a decision that I wanted to make, I would break out my arsenal and go to work.

And when I am on a rampage, I am a force to be reckoned with because I don't back down. I could use my techniques for as long as it took for me to accomplish my goal and to get want I wanted.

So my tactics would simply wear him out. It was just too much work to deal with my bad attitude.

Consequently, my behavior built a wall of resentment in our relationship and our relationship remained stagnant for many years.

But when I began this journey I came to realize that I wasn't a Christian wife. Instead, I was a warden to a man that was living in a free society. And boy was I work! I challenged him on everything. My husband worked a full time job during the day and probably felt that he had to come home to work his other fulltime job--ME!. I may have gotten the satisfaction of having things my way but it came at the expense of having a close relationship with my husband. Because there is absolutely no way to have a close, intimate, mutually fulfilling relationship when one partner is self centered and focused on his/her own agenda. So as long as I continued to act like a child, my relationship with my husband did not flourish. It wasn't until God began ministering to me about becoming my husband's mistress that I began to self examine myself and look at the many areas that I needed to change. I realized that I already had the man I had always prayed for but I had changed him into another person because of my disrespectful approach towards and interactions with him.

I learned that my husband will never be willing to be the man of my dreams as long as I continued to disrespect him and dishonor his position as leader. As long as I think I know better than him and am a better decision maker than he is, he will always resent me and therefore never be willing to meet my needs.

So in an effort to make things right and put our

relationship on the right track I had to apologize to him for making him feel as though he had to follow my lead on every decision. I apologized for bringing a diva attitude into our marriage and disrespecting his position as head over our household. I apologized for not allowing him to be an individual and for trying to control every aspect of his life. I committed to respecting him and following his lead without interference. And I committed to honoring him as the gift that God had blessed me with.

If you can relate to my story, then you too must make the needed changes in an effort to save or revive your relationship. It will not be easy but change requires change.

My husband and I are still on our journey but things have definitely changed for the better and our relationship is finally experiencing some growth.

Respect >Love

"And let the wife see that she respects and reverences her husband [that she notices him, regards him, honors him, prefers him, venerates, and esteems him; and that she defers to him, praises him, and loves and admires him exceedingly]" Ephesians 5:33b (AMP).

The Apostle Paul, the author of this text, didn't want wives to have to guess at what respecting their husbands meant. He took the time to lay it out in plain terms that could be understood by every wife and future wife. Everything women need to know about respecting their men is included inside of the parenthesis.

Respect means that you notice him. He is not an afterthought, a chore on the to-do list or an inconvenience to your life. You take notice of what he brings to the table. You notice him as a man and because he is your man he is given special attention. He feels special to you because you prefer him over everything else in your life right under your relationship with God. Respect means honoring his position as your husband and to hold him in high regards. Respect means telling him how awesome he is and showing great admiration for him.

Your husband's need for respect far outweighs his need to feel loved. He cannot function without your respect. He cannot excel without your respect. He cannot heal without your respect. That's why the bible doesn't command you to love him. It commands you to respect him. Stop trying to prove to your husband that you love him. Spending time with him, buying him gifts or doing thoughtful things for him are the things that you like when someone is communicating love towards you. While your husband probably appreciates your acts of love, he would prefer more acts of respect.

Any disrespect towards your husband will make the relationship stale and unfulfilling. Disrespectful actions, words, and facial expressions are all weapons that have the ability of crushing your husband's love towards you. That's because it is very difficult to express love towards someone when you feel as if that person doesn't respect you.

That is the reason why you are feeling cheated in your marriage. You feel that you cook for him, clean for him, run his errands, take care of his kids, etc and he still doesn't respond to you in a loving way. It could be that he doesn't feel as if you respect him.

Dr. Emerson Eggrich tells us in his book, Love and Respect, that when women feel unloved, we naturally act disrespectfully. And when husbands feel disrespected, they naturally act unloving. This concept is absolutely true! You don't respect him because you don't feel loved by him. He doesn't show you love because he doesn't feel respected by you. That is what Dr. Eggrich calls the "crazy cycle" in marriages and our job is to break the cycle before it ruins our relationship.

When you show disrespect towards your spouse it causes him to question his manhood and ability to be the leader of his home. Disrespect is like knocking the wind out of him and he will walk around defeated and deflated. He will question his decisions and adequacy. He won't attempt to be more than he is because he will doubt his abilities. This will cause you to become frustrated with him because he has no direction for you and the family. He won't be able to articulate clear goals for you and he will defer to you to make decisions even regarding the simplest things. Consequently, you will get overwhelmed because you have to make every decision. And the relationship will disintegrate to the point where you begin questioning if you can live with a man that cannot make a decision on his own.

Conversely, respect has the opposite effect. Respect inflates your man's chest. Respect makes him feel like he can conquer the world. Respect makes him feel confident in his ability to lead his family and make sound decisions. Honor and respect are paramount to men. They can do without love but they cannot function or achieve their greatness without the respect of their women.

Respect Him as Your Man

As author Sharon Jaynes says in her book, Becoming the Woman of His Dreams, "respect is the one thing that he (your husband) can't do without."

The mistress is respectful in a way that gives her man confidence in his ability to become great in every area of his life.

A major area where you can show your husband respect is by respecting that he is an adult.

You don't need to play the role of God or try to be his conscious. If your husband is involved in certain activities that you don't agree with, stop nagging him about them. It is God's job to deal with your husband on those issues. Accept the fact that you are not God and you can't do enough crying, yelling, or cursing to get him to stop the activities that he wants to be involved in. Your husband will find a way to continue his involvement in those activities until he decides that he wants something different in his life.

God is the only One that can change the heart of a person.

Playing detective, gathering facts, and committing your energy to prove his guilt will drive you crazy. Let him be a man. Let him be an individual. The best thing you can do is go to God's throne on his behalf asking that God does the necessary work to get your husband on the right track.

Another way to show respect is to value his opinions/advice in different situations and use his feedback to make a decision. Respect means respecting his ideas, opinions and thoughts. It means allowing him to be your man and not trying to overthrow him as head of the household. When you show respect to your man, it invigorates him. It lets him know that he is capable of making good decisions. It makes him feel adequate and sufficient. It puts wind in his sails and allows him to fly to new heights. Stop shooting down his ideas. Stop making him feel unimportant or like his opinion doesn't matter. Both of those actions are disrespectful. Let him be your man. Let him be the man. I am not saying that you shouldn't express your opinions or concerns or become a mindless robot who does everything that she is told. I am proposing that you learn to be an effective communicator without being disrespectful, dismissive or doubtful about your husband's ability to make a sound decision.

"I want so badly for my wife to respect me. I know that I have messed up in the past and don't deserve her respect but I want it anyway. It haunts me that she won't respect my opinions or value my thoughts. I think about it day and night. I cry about it, get angry about it and try to show her that I am worthy of her respect. But nothing seems to change. I would give anything for her to just show me respect. I would love her more and feel closer to her if she gave me some respect."

Showing your husband unconditional respect is a must for a healthy marriage. In his book, Dr. Eggrich goes on to say that men shouldn't have to earn the respect of their wives no more than wives should have to earn the love of their husbands. Women should show respect towards their husbands simply because they are married to them. Husbands shouldn't have to prove to their wives that they are worthy of our respect. They shouldn't have to accomplish certain tasks to earn respect. Giving respect isn't based on actions or inactions. Respect is based on position as a husband. Respect comes with the title of husband and God sees the two as interconnected. You cannot have one without the other. You cannot have a great husband if you refuse to respect him.

I once heard Author Michelle McKinney Hammond say that a man's secretary gives him what he wants not what she thinks he needs. His secretary must show him respect in order to keep her job. She isn't forcing her opinions on him. She defers to him and is happy to give him what he asks for. She looks to him for guidance and direction. She is kind and respectful. She doesn't argue with the boss and she stays in her role without crossing boundaries. In their work relationship, he calls the shots. That is probably the reason men often have affairs with their secretaries. If he is constantly being mistreated and disrespected by his wife, but being built up and validated by his secretary, then his relationship with his wife becomes less of a priority.

Your husband will never try to meet your needs or to make you happy if you refuse to show respect in the way you talk to and treat him. And he will not attempt to achieve his goals because his confidence in himself will be shaken. After all, if the woman who promised to love, honor and cherish him doesn't find anything respectable about him, how will the rest of the world? He can only become great due to your influence including your respectful behavior towards him.

Disrespect and Anger

Your disrespect of your husband may also be the reason for his anger. If you have noticed that your husband seems angry or hard to get along with or argues with you about little things, it may be that he feels as if you don't respect him.

During the times when I was acting in a disrespectful way towards my husband, I noticed that he would withdraw and not have much to say to me. He would also get upset by the most insignificant things. He didn't feel close to me and most of the time didn't want to be near me. It wasn't until I began to become mature enough to realize that the distance I felt between us was the result of how disrespectful I was to him. Likewise, respect may be the key that unlocks the door of anger and resentment that your husband feels towards you.

Deferring is respectful

Wives can also show respect by deferring to their husbands. A wife may be asked to make a certain decision but because she isn't in a position of ultimate authority and doesn't bear ultimate responsibility, she will often need to defer to what her husband thinks should be done in the situation.

"And the LORD God commanded the man, "You are free to eat from any tree in the garden; but you must not eat from the tree of the knowledge of good and evil, for when you eat from it you will certainly die." When the woman saw that the fruit of the tree was good for food and pleasing to the eye, and also desirable for gaining wisdom, she took some and ate it. She also gave some to her husband, who was with her, and he ate it. Then the man and his wife heard the sound of the LORD God as he was walking in the garden in the cool of the day, and they hid from the LORD God among the trees of the garden. But the LORD God called to the man,

"Where are you?" The man said, "The woman you put here with me—she gave me some fruit from the tree, and I ate it." Then the LORD God said to the woman, "What is this you have done?" To Adam he said, "Because you listened to your wife and ate fruit from the tree about which I commanded you, 'You must not eat from it,' "Cursed is the ground because of you; through painful toil you will eat food from it all the days of your life. It will produce thorns and thistles for you, and you will eat the plants of the field. By the sweat of your brow you will eat your food until you return to the ground, since from it you were taken; for dust you are and to dust you will return." Genesis 2:16-17, 3:6, 8-9, 11-13a, 17-19 (NIV)

Instead of approaching Adam, Satan approached Eve to make a decision about whether or not to disobey the command of God. It was Eve who was tempted and decided to disobey God and offered the fruit to her husband. But when God showed up, he didn't call Eve's name, He called Adam and questioned Adam, as leader of the family, about the decision that was made. So this teaches us that if anything goes wrong within the family, the husband bears the responsibility for the outcome. That is the reason that wives need to respect their husbands' decisions, even if we don't agree with them.

What Eve should have done was to tell Satan "let me talk to my husband about it first and see what he has to say on this matter." Not because she couldn't make a decision but out of respect for Adam as her husband.

But because she didn't take the time to discuss this issue with Adam and made a decision based on what she thought was best, there were serious consequences.

And you wonder why your husband doesn't want to follow your lead?

Ladies, you were never intended to lead the family. That is why God created Adam, gave him a job and responsibilities, gave him the command to stay away from the tree, then gave him a wife. But because you want things done your way, in your time and don't have time to wait for your husband to make a decision, you often put everything God is trying to do with your husband in jeopardy. A lot of wives and their attitudes are the very reasons why we haven't seen changes in our men. We are too busy showing them what they should be doing if they were 'real men'.

By her actions, a wife often tells her man that a 'real man' doesn't take too long to make a decision. A 'real man' doesn't have any issues coming up with a solution to a problem. And we constantly take on the role of being a 'real man' which #1 alienates our husbands and causes them to rebel against us and #2 pushes God over into the passenger seat while we drive ourselves where we want to go.

God gave Adam the command and Adam informed his wife Eve of what God wanted them to do. We know that she was fully aware of the direction that her husband gave her because she was able to tell the serpent what the command was. Yet, she decided to act independently and also brought her husband along down the path of disobedience.

Now I know that this respect and deferment thing is a new concept for a lot of us. But we must get it ladies. These are areas where we cannot afford to continue to miss the mark.

Your husband may only be spiritually mature enough to receive basic instructions from God. He may not be able to receive big instructions at this time in his life. God could be talking to your husband privately regarding how he treats you, how he leads you, the marriage, his relationship with God and other things that you have been praying about. He doesn't need you to be in his face telling him to do something different than what God told him to do. He may be struggling with just following God's basic instructions to him.

We can guess that if Adam ate so freely of the apple that Eve offered him, then he must have been already struggling with the temptation to disobey God's command. Think about it. No one can get you to do something that you have absolutely no interest in doing. You can only be tempted and led astray if what is being offered is tempting to you. For example, no one can tempt me to eat Brussels sprouts. No matter how well you have cooked them or how delicious you make them sound, I have no interest in eating them. I don't care about any of the health benefits related to eating them, I simply don't want them. On the other hand, if you offer me a chocolate chip cookie, then you've tempted me to partake of something that is already hard for me to resist. I know that I shouldn't eat the cookie because it has no nutritional value and will make me fat. And even if the doctor told me to stop eating sweets, when you offer a cookie to me I may not be able to resist that particular temptation. I may have only been able to stay the course of good health for as long as I stayed away from chocolate chip cookies. But as soon as you offered me a cookie, all of the things that the doctor said would go out of the window. That's because I was tempted in an area where I was already weak. That is what happened to Adam. His wife assisted Satan to get her husband to sin against God. She tempted her husband in an area that he wasn't strong enough to resist.

So as a wife, when your husband is already struggling in a certain area where he is trying to make positive changes, no matter how small those changes may be, you need to let God be God and stop using your own methods to get the changes you want.

If your husband says he wants to go to bible study, don't tell him that you want him to spend time with you that night. If he tells you that he is trying to stop smoking, don't bring him cigarettes trying to be nice to him. As his wife and life partner, you need to get out of the habit of presenting roadblocks so God can make the changes that you have been praying about.

Respect His Position

I know that some of you are asking the question "what if my husband doesn't have a relationship with God, am I still expected to follow his lead?" This is where a lot of women miss the mark.

I truly believe that wives aren't getting what we want out of our marriages because we don't know when to sit down, when to back down or when to shut up and let our men lead us.

The answer to that question is that God expects you to respect your husband just as you respect your boss at work or your pastor at church. It doesn't matter how spiritually, emotionally, financially or relationally immature your husband may be, you are called to be under his leadership and to respect his role as the head of the household. And becoming the head is not dictated by who makes the most money. The way the hierarchy is structured is, God gives directions to the husband, the husband gives leadership and direction to the wife and the wife helps her husband with leading the kids. God----- husband-----wife.

I want to answer that question another way. I want you to consider an organizational structure or the structure of a church.

In an organization, there is the CEO who supervises and leads the COO. The COO supervises and leads the Director and the Director supervises and leads the other managers. In a church setting, the Pastor leads the Associate Pastor, and the Associate Pastor leads the Pastoral Leadership Team. If the CEO or Pastor, as heads of the organization, can't make it to work for some reason, it is the job of the COO or Associate Pastor to make a decision that lines up with the goals of their leader. The person making the decision must ensure that he/she makes decisions that are in line with what he/she has been trained to do.

So if your husband is not getting his directions directly from God, then it is your job to get directions from God with the understanding that just because you are in direct contact with God doesn't mean that you have been promoted to your husband's position as leader. Even when your husband is spiritually absent and/or spiritually immature, he still holds the same position in the household and his position calls for respect by those positioned beneath him. The only time that it is permissible to step out of line with your husband is when he directs you to do something that is against God's principles, are illegal or immoral.

Just like in any business. If the COO or Associate Pastor asks the people that they are in charge of to do something unethical or illegal, the people given the instructions are not obligated to comply. If your husband is leading you down an illegal or immoral path, don't follow him. Otherwise, the expectation is that the wife follows the leadership of her husband regardless of his relationship with God.

Undivided Attention is a sign of respect

Luke 10:38-42 says

"As Jesus and his disciples were on their way, he came to a village where a woman named Martha opened her home to him. She had a sister called Mary, who sat at the Lord's feet listening to what he said. But Martha was distracted by all the preparations that had to be made. She came to him and asked, "Lord, don't you care that my sister has left me to do the work by myself? Tell her to help me!"

"Martha, Martha," the Lord answered, "you are worried and upset about many things, but few things are needed—or indeed only one. Mary has chosen what is better, and it will not be taken away from her."

Martha was too busy ensuring that everything was perfect in the household and risked missing the opportunity to spend time with him. She was so busy making preparations that she didn't take the time to listen to what he had to say. Mary, on the other hand, stopped everything she was doing as soon as Jesus walked in the door. She didn't care that there were dishes that still needed to be washed. She didn't care that there was food that still needed to be prepared. She showed Jesus the ultimate respect by giving Him her full, undivided attention. And with this decision, she pleased Jesus greatly.

Don't we wives often act like Martha? We are so busy making sure that the laundry is complete, the meals are prepared, the dishes are washed, etc that we don't even notice or care when our husbands make it home. Our husbands would be lucky to get a kiss hello from us much less a listening ear and undivided attention. But as shown by this example, undivided attention for a man shows him that you respect him and that you are interested in what he has to say.

Chapter 8

The Mistress is Quiet and Humble

Ladies, Ladies, Ladies. Is there ever a time when we don't have something negative to say to or about our husbands? Is there ever a time when we give our husbands a break from all of the nagging, complaining or arguing even if they are the reason for our complaints? If you are like me then the answer to that question is "No". Well, I wouldn't exactly say that I never give my husband a break; I would say that I rarely give my husband a break. In fact, I can find something to say about almost anything or any situation and have been known to offer my opinion on any subject, whether solicited or unsolicited. And according to the book of Proverbs I am not the only wife that doesn't know how to keep quiet.

The book of Proverbs was written by King Solomon and seems to be the king's own personal journal where he documented his experiences.

With 1000 wives and girlfriends in his life, I believe that it is safe to say that King Solomon had more than his fair share of relationship issues. There was probably not a day that went by that he didn't have an issue with a woman. Either a woman was complaining, finding fault, or arguing with him about something he did or something he said.

Look at what this old wise king had to say regarding

relationships and women.

"It is better to dwell in a corner of the housetop [on the flat oriental roof, exposed to all kinds of weather] than in a house shared with a nagging, quarrelsome, and faultfinding woman." Proverbs 21:9 (AMP)

"Better to live in a desert than with a quarrelsome and nagging wife." Proverbs 21:19 (AMP)

"A wife of noble character is her husband's crown, but a disgraceful wife is like decay in his bones." Proverbs 12:4 (NIV)

"A quarrelsome wife is like the dripping of a leaky roof in a rainstorm; restraining her is like restraining the wind or grasping oil with the hand." Proverbs 27:15-16 (NIV).

King Solomon says that it would be better for husbands to live on the roof top exposed to rain, snow, hail and natural disasters than to live with their wives when wives become argumentative, fault finding or nagging! Or better yet, he suggests that maybe husbands should seek refuge in a desert, an environment that has the potential of killing him within days, than to stay in the same house contending with us!

He even compares an angry woman to the dripping of a leaky roof on a rainy day. Can you hear it? Plop. Plop. Plop. Plop. Unbelievable!

I have had men tell me that there is nothing sexier than a woman who knows when to shut her mouth. A woman that doesn't always have to have the last word and keeps her negative opinions to herself is a woman that has no trouble keeping a man. Ladies, let's face it. There is nothing sexy, desirable or admirable about the things we allow to come from our mouths. We can build people up and tear them down all in the same sentence.

"I'm scared of my wife's mouth. I am no match for her when we get into an argument. She has a way with words and always makes me feel like I am wrong, even when I know that I am right."

The way this husband feels is not unique. I have talked to several husbands who run for the door when their wives go on a rampage. Our mouths should be the aphrodisiac that turns our men on but we often use our mouths, not to stimulate our men's bodies, but to demean, nag and criticize.

But I know what some of you are thinking right now. You are saying to yourself "I'm not that bad. These passages of scripture don't apply to me." Well, I have news for you my friend-- yes you can be that bad and yes those scriptures do apply to you. We have all complained, nagged and found some fault in our husbands at one time or another during our relationships. There is no doubt about that. And all women tend to become a little too much to handle when something is bothering us. When those times occur we have the tendency to lash out at our husbands with as much intensity and passion as we think necessary to get our points across and to send them a clear message that the situation better not happen again. So we are all that bad sometimes.

But a Proverbs 31 woman doesn't behave like that. A Proverbs 31 woman has a quiet spirit, a spirit of peace, and a spirit of gentleness.

S.U.S

"Wives, in the same way submit yourselves to your own husbands so that, if any of them do not believe the word, they may be won over without words by the behavior of their wives, when they see the purity and reverence of your lives.

Your beauty should not come from outward adornment, such as elaborate hairstyles and the wearing of gold jewelry or fine clothes. Rather, it should be that of your inner self, the unfading beauty of a gentle and quiet spirit, which is of great worth in God's sight" 1 Peter 3:1-4 (NIV).

Haven't you noticed that you have been talking to your husband about the same issues for years and he hasn't changed yet? That's because your words will never change him. But we think we know better, so we keep following our own techniques instead of doing what God has instructed us to do. If God says to be quiet then we need to be quiet. He knows men. He is one of them and he created the rest of them. So if the Head Man in charge is telling you how to get your man to change, you should listen up. Besides, men who walked with God and given inspiration and guidance by God and used by God to accomplish great things on earth are clearly able to express what they need and desire from their women. And Peter, the author of the above scripture, thought it necessary to tell wives how to interact with their husbands and how to inspire their husbands to change. According to Peter, the keys to success are: learning to close our mouths, living pure and reverent lives, and adopting a gentle and quiet spirit. That is the winning formula.

So for the sake of marriages everywhere, the therapist in me is begging the wife in all of us to please learn, accept and practice the acronym S.U.S.

S.U.S. stands for Shut Up Sometimes. Just shut up!

I know it's HARD because those men just keep doing things that we don't understand. If they would just make better decisions, we wouldn't have to complain all of the time. I know sister. I feel your pain.

Maybe we can form a married mistress support group to help us get through this. I can see it now. All of the wives sitting in a circle at a S.U.S. group session trying to stay on the wagon by looking to our peers for support. The beginning of the session begins with each wife introducing herself and admitting that she has a problem. Hello, I am Dee Johnson and I admit that I am a fault finding, complaining, and argumentative wife.

Ok. Ok. I got a little off track but you get the point. I am simply saying that each wife must learn to control her tongue by any means necessary. You may have to have a group of lady friends or accountability partners that you can vent to so you don't have to voice your complaints directly to your husband. Let me be clear, if you decide to go that route, make sure that your venting doesn't turn into husband bashing. I am totally against anymore husband bashing sessions. I firmly believe that you cannot ask God to build up what you are tearing down with your tongue. So for that reason, please ensure that while you vent your frustrations or concerns to others you are careful not to demean, demolish or damage your husband's reputation or character. You can take those types of complaints directly to God.

Whatever you need to do to ensure that you aren't always complaining, arguing or finding fault with your husband, needs to be done quickly. Our mouths are meant to exhort, encourage, and excite our men and shouldn't be used as a lethal weapon against them. The time has come when we must take responsibility for our own actions and stop using our husband's flaws as a reason why we don't control our tongues.

Using Discernment

Wives must also master the art of deciphering the appropriate time to speak from the appropriate time to be quiet. We don't always need to say exactly what we're thinking. We need to think through what is on our minds, weigh the benefits and consequences of our words and filter our thoughts through prayer before we approach our men with any concerns. Then we need to tailor our approach while we talk to them.

Look at what King Solomon had to say about Mrs. 31.

"She opens her mouth in skillful and godly Wisdom, and on her tongue is the law of kindness [giving counsel and instruction]" Proverbs 31:26 (AMP).

He goes on to say the following about women in general:

"A gracious and good woman wins honor [for her husband]" Proverbs 11:16a (AMP)

"A wise, understanding, and prudent wife is from the Lord." Proverbs 19:14b (AMP)

Those are the words that I want my husband to use when he describes me. I don't want him to feel safer on top of a roof or in a desert. I don't want him to feel like I am decay that causes his bones to rot. I want to be known as a virtuous wife that has enough wisdom to know when to speak and when to be quiet.

Below are some suggestions about deciding the appropriate time to keep quiet and the appropriate time to speak.

When to be quiet:

When your husband wants to vent or voice frustration

When you are angry with him and feel like cursing the day he was born

When he is angry with you

When you have hurtful or damaging words about him running through your mind

Whenever you have the urge to say "I told you so"

When to speak:

When he ask for your advice or opinion

When you need to pray with him about any concern

When you are concerned about a particular situation

After you have prayed and gathered your thoughts

When you are calm

When you have the right spirit (not a contentious, bitter, angry or vengeful spirit)

The Role of the Ego

The reasons why we won't shut our mouths or watch

our words is all rooted in pride.

We think we know better and can make better choices. So we make it a practice of constantly telling our husbands what they are doing wrong, how little time they are spending with us and how they loaded the dishwasher incorrectly. We bring up the past because it bears some resemblance to the present and we lay out a case pointing to his guilt. We put him on trial for the past, the present and for what may happen in the future. And because we don't practice the art of being quiet, we often hurt our husbands, make them feel inadequate and consequently they begin to harbor negative emotions and resentment towards us. We think we can say whatever is on our minds whenever we want and they just have to deal with it. And we continue to be driven by this entitlement mentality. We think we are entitled to be loud, disrespectful and rude because in our own eyes we can do no wrong. Or if we have done something wrong, what we have done pales in comparison to what our husbands have done.

Pride tells us that they should do everything they can to make up for their mistakes and for hurting us. But we are often disappointed that they are incapable or unwilling to bow down to us and do everything in their power to show how sorry they are and how committed they have become to improve our relationship.

So our pride leads us to become resentful, judgmental, more intolerant and louder thinking these techniques will make them do what's right in our sight. And year after year we are frustrated because we keep chasing this illusion and they keep disappointing us.

The ego is the driving force behind all of this madness.

Author Wayne Dyer uses the acronym E.G.O. to mean "Edging God Out". As you allow pride to dominate your heart and mind, the ego grows larger. And as your words, thoughts and actions "edge God out" it also alienates your husband.

After a while you will find yourself in a lonely marriage, sleeping next to someone who can barely stand to look at you. Because there is no way to operate in pride and get godly results. You cannot continue to act like a lawyer, judge and jury to convict your husband of crimes you think he has committed. Most of you are not prosecutors or district attorneys and you don't need to lay out a case to convict your husband and find him guilty based on his history and the evidence against him. Learn to release your husband from his past mistakes. To hold him hostage to his past is your ego at work. Like Author and speaker Maya Angelo says "love liberates, it doesn't hold onto. To hold onto is ego." If you truly love your husband and want the best from your marriage to him, set him free.

Practice Humility

The mistress humbles herself when she is with her man because she realizes that she isn't in competition with him. She doesn't need to go toe to toe, ensuring she is right all of the time. She doesn't create a combat zone. Instead, she practices humility in an effort to allow him to be the man in their relationship. She sets it up to make him feel like he is in control and holds the cards in the relationship. She remains humble even when she doesn't agree with him because it's not important for her to be right. It's important to her to get her needs met.

Likewise, you also must learn to practice humility in all of your interactions with your husband. You can begin doing this by constantly filtering your words.

Before opening your mouth ask yourself the following three questions:

1. What is my true motivation for bringing up this issue? Am I doing it to show him that he was wrong? Am I doing it so I can feel like I am right?

2. Is what I am about to say necessary for the growth and development of my marital relationship? If yes, have I already said these things to him in the past? If yes, why am I bringing it up again? If no, do I really need to bring it up?

3. Will discussing this issue help us move forward in our relationship?

By asking yourself these questions, you will be surprised to see that almost half of the conversations that you intend to have with your husband will be diminished. That is because half of the time, the only reason that we bring up issues is due to our egos and wanting to feel like we are right about something.

Chapter 9

The Mistress is Fun

My husband loves to play basketball. If given the opportunity he would play on a daily basis. And for the past 3 years he has driven approximately 50 miles roundtrip for a chance to engage in his favorite recreational activity with a group of guys he has formed friendships with. And even though my husband doesn't mind driving 40 minutes each way to play basketball, it never made sense to me to use all of that time and gas to go play a sport that he can play up the street from our house at the local gym. And to make matters worse, the games are always on a weekday. But for whatever reason my husband doesn't mind the drive or the time it takes to get there.

During half time all of the men have bible study together. So you would think that I would be pushing him out of the door each week. But not me. Even though I know he loves to go and will get the opportunity to hear God's word, because it doesn't make sense to me that he drives so far and stays gone so long, I usually try to convince him to stay home with me.

For my husband, having me accompany him to watch him play has always been his preference. If he had it his way, I would be there every Tuesday night as he tries to impress me with his basketball skills.

But as I mentioned before, I never do anything that I am

not interested in doing.

The reason that I don't usually accompany him to the gym every week is because it is an inconvenience to me. When I get out of traffic after working all day, traveling an additional 40 minutes isn't attractive to me. Besides, I want to be in bed at a descent hour so I can be ready for work the next morning without feeling tired. But my husband usually doesn't come home before 10:30pm. Consequently, I only go to the gym with him maybe 4 times per year.

Now, chances are, that if my husband had gone to play basketball during our dating years, I would have gone with him a lot more often. As his girlfriend, I would have made it a point to be there every Tuesday night, rain, sleet, snow, or hurricane, no matter how tired I was. And if there was another woman at the gym who was interested in getting to know my man, I would have found the energy to be there every week to ensure she didn't make a move on him. In fact, I would have never missed a basketball night. That's because I hadn't closed the deal on our relationship yet and needed to keep my suitor interested in me.

But as a wife, I feel as if I can pick and choose whether or not I will show up to support my husband and cheer him on to victory. And that is the problem. Typically, once we have been promoted from girlfriend to wife, we develop this mentality of "I've already got him so I don't have to fight for something that is already mine. He's not going anywhere because he is committed to me so I don't have to work as hard to keep him." And that, my friend, is the wrong mindset to have when it comes to marriage. In fact, no wife should ever stop working on her marital relationship. A wise woman recognizes that her deal is never secure; not as long as there are other women walking this earth. No wife should ever believe that just because she can produce a wedding certificate that her marriage and relationship are secure.

In the book, His Needs Her Needs, Dr. William F. Harley, Jr. says "It is not uncommon for women, when they are single, to join men in pursuing their interest. They find themselves hunting, fishing, playing football, and watching movies they would never have chosen on their own. (But) After marriage wives often try to interest their husbands in activities more to their own liking. If their attempts fail, they may encourage their husbands to continue their recreational activities without them."

A wise wife understands that if her husband's needs for recreational companionship aren't being met by her, another woman, pretending to like the same activities he enjoys, can easily invade her territory and capture his attention. A wife has to learn to never be so comfortable in her relationship that she neglects to have fun with her husband. It is time for wives to get uncomfortable. We have been comfortable in our relationships for far too long. We need to go back to doing all of the things we did when we were dating and trying to convince them that we could meet their every need.

And as a mistress, you have to stop being such a bore. Stop being so uptight and serious. Do you have to be so responsible all of the time? Life cannot always be about bill paying, escorting the kids to various events and you being too tired to give your man a proper greeting when he comes home. You have to learn to stop doing things on your terms and according to what suits you. Learn to let your hair down and get a sense of adventure in your life. If you are bored and unfulfilled and seeking a thrill, chances are, so is your husband.

Sometimes because you are disappointed in or frustrated by your husband or because you don't see how important it is to have fun in your relationship, your zeal for having fun often gets tossed aside. But guess what? No matter how bad things are, he still desires to have some fun with the girl he married.

When is the last time you broke your own routine and did something spontaneous? When is the last time you kidnapped your husband from work and arranged to have a play date with him? Mistresses bring excitement to a man.

Ask yourself 'would I want to be married to me?' If you cannot answer with an enthusiastic YES, then don't expect your husband to be able to answer with an enthusiastic yes either. Yes, you may be a good housekeeper, mother, and cook but how good are you at being a playmate and friend to your husband? I'm sure your husband appreciates all of the things you do to keep the train moving forward for your family but I am also sure that your man desires a woman who is easy to get along with, has a laid back attitude, can laugh at herself and who can take a joke.

You must be willing to fulfill your husband's needs of having you as his recreational companion. And you need to be enthusiastic about doing so. You should be happy that he wants to enjoy your company and have you by his side. You didn't mind having fun before you got your wedding ring so don't change the script just because you have said "I do". I do simply means that you will do the things that are necessary to keep your marriage from faltering. I do means that you are committing to do the things that show your husband that his needs are important to you. Your husband wants to know that you are still the woman of his dreams. You know, the woman you were before the wedding vows were exchanged, before the kids came along, the one who couldn't get enough of him and who sought to make him happy. He is secretly praying that that woman will show up again. If you are dull, lifeless, and unwilling to have fun, then your marriage will end up in the marital graveyard.

So begin dating him again. Begin enjoying your husband's company. Become your husband's playmate. Have fun, wrestle, joke around. Be playful and less irritable. Be joyful and less critical. Isn't it funny that you didn't become uptight and sensitive until after you got married? Surely, if you had acted that way while you were dating, he never would have asked you to marry him. When you were dating, you weren't so sensitive and didn't read more into the things he said and did. Now that you're married you take everything as a personal offense or attack. Your husband cannot joke with you because you will turn things around and make him your enemy. So learn to keep things light. Unless you have indisputable proof that what he said or did was done with the intention of hurting you, let it go. Stop being so sensitive.

Find a new place to visit or a new activity to get involved in. Try something you've never tried before. Do something spontaneous, stop being so predictable.

I remember during the early stages of our dating relationship, we looked forward to watching The X-files every Sunday night. That was something that we both enjoyed doing as a couple. We went to church, ate, enjoyed the day and watched The X-files. That was our routine. It's time to get back to the things that make your relationship interesting again.

The mistress is so much fun that her man finds pure joy in being in her company. A mistress brings a sense of adventure and excitement to a relationship. She doesn't want her man to think of their relationship as boring or stale. The reason that he wants to be with her is because she brings something new and interesting to his life.

But There is No Money, No Time and I Don't Know What to do

When you make excuses, what you are really saying is

that your husband and your relationship aren't worth the effort. If that is the case, your marriage will never experience growth and you will never be happy with your husband.

I have counseled women who have said that they couldn't afford to do anything fun. Please understand that having fun isn't about spending a ton of money on something that is expensive. Having fun doesn't have to cost a dime. Watching X-files didn't cost me any more than I was going to spend on my cable bill anyway. Driving 40 minutes to the basketball gym cost about $4 in gas money. But the value of both of those things was priceless because they meant so much to my husband. Having fun is about enjoying each other's company. You can be flat broke and still have fun with your husband. Besides, paying to participate in a fun activity is cheaper than going through a divorce.

Here are a few fun, inexpensive ideas:

Have a picnic in the park

Go dancing

Play video games

Challenge him in a board game

Take turns reading poetry to each other

Have a candlelight dinner at home

Go for a hike

Ride bikes

Workout

Find a weekly TV show to watch

Wrestle

Play cards

My husband and I enjoy going to a local coffee shop and challenge each other to a game of checkers over a cup of our favorite blend of coffee. We also enjoy looking at really expensive homes and picking out what features we want to include in our future dream home.

You know your husband best so find a fun activity that both of you are likely to enjoy doing together.

I have heard other wives use the excuse that they don't know how to plan anything fun or special. My response to them is to use your creativity. I usually have them complete the following activity to get their creative juices flowing. I want you to complete the exercise as well.

On the lines below plan a simple vacation for you and your girlfriends. Include everything you need to do in order to make the trip possible. Give yourself a maximum of 10 minutes to complete this exercise. Use another sheet of paper if you need more room to write.

_____

_____

_____

_____

_____

_____

_____

_____

After completing this exercise, I am willing to bet that at least 75% of your plans for a vacation for you and your friends are complete. Am I right? Weren't you able to detail the majority of the things that need to be done prior to your trip? Things like getting a passport, arrange babysitting, put in a vacation request at work, purchase plane tickets and make hotel reservations are probably all included on your list. Maybe you put down that you need to save $50/month for the next few months as part of your plan so you can afford to go. That plan only took you 10 minutes to complete.

Isn't it interesting that you were able to plan a vacation for yourself and your friends but cannot come up with any ideas on how to plan something special with your spouse? Use that same ingenuity and creativity that you used during this exercise to plan something for your sweetheart.

Having little time and no money are not valid excuses. Will you have time for your husband after another woman enters the picture? Will you have time to see a marriage counselor when your marriage is on the brink of collapse? My advice to you is to make time for things that you deem important before trouble creeps into your relationship. You just learned that in 10 minutes you are able to detail everything you need to do to plan something special with your spouse.

But what about the kids?

What about them? Without your husband there would be no kids. The reason the kids were created was because you and your man found some uninterrupted alone time. So in an effort to become your husband's mistress, you must get rid of the kids sometimes. Yes, your role as a mother is important. Yes, you should do whatever you can to raise good kids with good morals. But as a wife, your role as a mom is secondary. Your marriage is your primary ministry and should be your primary relationship. Your husband should never feel like an afterthought and only get your leftovers. One day it could lead to you and the kids being together ---- alone. The kids will not be traumatized simply because you didn't give them all of your time and energy every single day of their lives. They may try to manipulate you and attempt to make you feel guilty about it but don't fall for it. Your kids will be just fine without you hovering over them for a few hours or even a few days. Cut the cord already. Distance makes the heart grow fonder.

Since your marriage is your primary relationship here on earth you must invest sufficient time and energy in ensuring that your relationship stays strong. Date nights are a must. Designated, uninterrupted time together is a must. Time to reconnect with your husband is a must. Sex is a must. Getting time away from the kids is a must. The reason the mistress seems so appealing is because usually there aren't kids interfering with her man's time and attention. She can focus all of her attention on him.

So go ahead, get a babysitter, and plan a special day of fun with your husband.

And don't wait until it's too late to begin this process. Don't wait until another woman enters the picture before you decide to fight for your man. You need to begin fighting from the beginning of the relationship. You must make your relationship a priority.

Chapter 10

The Mistress is Independent

Trying to maintain total independence while attempting to enjoy an intimate relationship with my husband was absolutely impossible. As an independent woman, I did things my way, when I decided to do them and took as long as I pleased to get them done. But I soon learned that is the wrong mindset to bring into a marriage.

My husband and I were no longer two but one flesh in the eyes of God. What that means is that although both he and I have individual needs, responsibilities and desires, we cannot attempt to fulfill those areas at the exclusion of the other person in our relationship.

You and your husband may have similar callings from God. You may be working together in a ministry or vocation and that is perfectly fine. But as individuals you both also have been designated to accomplish other things outside of your relationship with your spouse. Just because you enter into a relationship with your husband doesn't mean that you should lose some of your individuality.

So when I say that the mistress is independent I simply mean that she has some separation from her husband at times so that she can accomplish what God has created her to accomplish.

Independence requires that you have your own identity apart from your relationship. It is vitally important for the health of your relationship that you give your husband space to work on accomplishing his individual goals. And it is equally important that you take time so you can work on accomplishing your individual goals. You are more than your husband's wife. You are more than the mother to his children. You are more than a daughter, friend, housekeeper, bill payer, or counselor. You have your own individual assignment that has been given to you by God. So take the time to invest in yourself. Spend some time with yourself to evaluate what is important to you. What are you passionate about? What interests do you have outside of your family life? How would you like to spend your free time? Spend time with your friends. Take a class for leisure or to further your education. Dare to dream a bigger dream for yourself. You cannot be everything to everyone else and neglect your needs, dreams and desires.

It is not selfish to take an interest in yourself. It is not selfish to work towards fulfilling your dreams or pursuing your passion. The world needs what you have to offer. God needs what you have to offer. God didn't give you gifts and talents for you to sit and wait for a better time to use them. With time, those unused gifts and talents will fade, not grow stronger. You were created to fulfill a specific void in this world and you are the only one that is able to do it in the way God envisioned. Keeping your gifts and talents to yourself is a disservice to you and to others. So don't sacrifice your gifts by refusing to use what God entrusted you with to fulfill a higher purpose.

And don't wait until the kids are grown and have left the house. Your needs cannot and shouldn't wait that long to be met. Of course, you have responsibilities as a wife and mother and you should fulfill those responsibilities. But you can fulfill those obligations without sacrificing yourself in the process.

And if you have settled into comfortable or familiar roles because you are unsure of what your calling is or what you have been created to do, then you need to spend much time in prayer seeking direction from God.

Codependency is not cute

Dear wife, please understand that just because your husband has something to do or has an outside interest beyond your relationship doesn't mean he is choosing the activity over spending time with you.

I have struggled with this a lot over the years. If my husband wanted to go play basketball when I wanted him to spend time with me, I would accuse him of putting his desire to have fun ahead of our relationship. If he wanted to hang out with the guys and I wanted him to do something for me, I would accuse him of putting his friends ahead of my needs. And on and on the accusations would go. But in my husband's eyes, he was just doing something that he thought was fun. For me, it was him being inconsiderate of me and not as committed to the relationship as I was.

Likewise, your husband may just see his activities as something that he wants to participate in. It doesn't mean that he is putting its importance above the importance of his relationship with you. So stop trying to make him feel guilty for wanting or needing to do things apart from you. Everything he does cannot be about you all of the time. In order to grow as a person and fulfill your God given roles in life, you both must maintain some individuality. Otherwise, how would you both learn from other experiences and apply what you have learned to your marital relationship and other areas of your life?

Codependency is not cute. Codependency is draining. Always wanting to be near, in the face of or in the space of your husband may be more than he wants to deal with. Your husband cannot spend every waking moment with you. He cannot be with you as often as you would like. He is busy doing what needs to be done as a husband, father and leader of his household. And some of those activities don't involve you. Learn to accept and be okay with that. You cannot find your identity in your husband.

I haven't met many men that want a woman that is clingy and has nothing else going for herself. Men are generally attracted to women who have a fulfilling life outside of their relationships with their men. So make sure you are a woman of substance and that you have outside interest that make you feel whole and complete.

That doesn't mean to treat your husband as if you don't need him because every man needs to feel needed. But have activities, hobbies and goals outside of your relationship with him where you can spend your time and energy. You will find that the more time you spend pursuing your dreams, passions and life work you will spend less time thinking about how unfulfilled you are in your relationship.

There are many wives who are discontent in their marriage because they simply have too much time on their hands and do nothing but ponder what is wrong in their relationships. A busy person doesn't have interest or energy to focus on how bad things are. So a simple solution for some marital issues is for an (un)busy wife to find something productive and meaningful to do with her day.

The Proverbs 31 woman had a lot of things going on that were independent of her marital relationship. While her husband was in the city making things happen, Mrs. 31 was in the town making things happen. She was busy running her household, buying properties, sewing, helping the needy and selling garments. She was entirely too busy to be codependent on her husband. Instead she ensured he was able to do what he needed to do so she could focus on what she needed to do. She wasn't interested in sitting at home all day, waiting on her husband to get home. She knew that God called her to be more than a wife and mother and she worked every day to fulfill her life's work.

A mistress understands that her man has a life outside of his relationship with her and doesn't attempt to force him to be her everything at the exclusion of other areas in his life.

Say 'No' Sometimes

If you are dissatisfied with the direction that your life is taking, it's up to you to change course. Don't stifle yourself just so others can flourish. There are times when you have to say 'No' to others and say 'Yes' to yourself.

As you learn to have balance in your life and learn the art of making your needs a priority, you will find that you have the extra time to pursue your interest and dreams. Being a balanced, independent woman allows you to be in the mindset of a mistress. But if you are overwhelmed with life, you will never be able to transition to a mistress because you will simply be too burned out to do so.

Get comfortable with setting firm boundaries with others. Learn that it is okay to tell them

I will not babysit your children;

I will not loan you money;

I will not bake a cake for your special event;

I will not style your hair for free.

If you think that doing those things will come at the expense of being true to yourself or if they will require more of you than you want to give away, then don't do them.

You know when you need a break. You know when you need a vacation. No one else will take the time to take care of you. It is your responsibility to yourself and to God to take care of your needs. God can get the best from you when you are not running on fumes. So don't feel guilty for taking care of your emotional, spiritual, mental, physical or financial needs. Those people that you had to say no to in order to save yourself, will be just fine.

And don't feel obligated to provide an explanation about your refusal to do what others are requesting of you. If you want to provide an explanation because it makes you feel more comfortable to explain yourself, then say something like "I don't have time; I have some personal things I need to get done; I'm not in a financial position to loan money or to give my services away for free anymore; I need to use my time to help my husband ensure that the needs of our family are being met.

Chapter 11

The Mistress is Financially Savvy

No man wants to be weighed down by the burden of debt. And no man wants a woman that bleeds him to a financial death. So a married mistress is not only a working woman but also a financially wise woman. Every wife needs to learn to respect the money her husband makes and stop spending everything she has on things that don't matter. Begin to treat money as a resource that allows you and your family to have freedom from the pressures of life. Learn to value money for the peace it can provide.

The Bible's View of Debt

I realize that this topic is not sexy or popular. But there are some topics that need to be addressed even when we'd rather not hear about them. This is one of those topics. The reason I have decided to include it is because I feel that it is necessary that you learn how to open the hand of God to get the financial blessings that you have been promised when you are in covenant with Him. So as Nike would say, let's "just do it".

I want to begin by discussing a few important things regarding the issue of financial debt.

1. It is not biblical and not God's perfect will for your family to be in debt.

"You will lend to many nations but will borrow from none. The LORD will make you the head, not the tail. If you pay attention to the commands of the LORD your God that I give you this day and carefully follow them, you will always be at the top, never at the bottom." Deuteronomy 28:12-13 (NIV).

You cannot position your household to be a lender if all of your credit cards are maxed out, your credit score is horrible and you are sinking from the weight of debt. And more importantly, you cannot be a mistress if you and your husband are stressed about debt because the debt will become a burden to both of you. And no one feels sexy when they are burdened.

2. "Every wise woman builds her house, but the foolish one tears it down with her own hands." Proverbs 14:1 (AMP).

A woman that makes foolish financial decisions is destined to always be a borrower and is contributing to the financial ruin of her family. It is silly to get your hair and nails done or to go shopping for clothes when you haven't even paid your bills yet. A wise wife knows that the needs of her family and household are far more important than ensuring that she tries to keep up with the Joneses.

Proverbs 31:25b (AMP) says "she rejoices over the future [the latter day or time to come, knowing that she and her family are in readiness for it]!"

Mrs. 31 didn't worry about how the bills would get

paid. She didn't worry if the finances were enough to meet the needs of her family. Mrs.31 ensured that her family was prepared for whatever happened. She prepared ahead of time by saving and investing her resources wisely. She recognized that having financial security would free her and her husband from the worry of having to work longer hours in an effort to get more money.

Proverbs 31:14 says "she brings food from a far country."

This says to me that she bargains shops to ensure she finds the best deals with the highest quality. She may have to drive across town but if it means that she is getting a great deal once she factors in time and gas, she will did so.

3. "Will a mere mortal rob God? Yet you rob Me. But you ask, How are we robbing you? In tithes and offerings. You are under a curse—your whole nation—because you are robbing Me."Malachi 3:8-10 (NIV)

God's intention for each of his children is that they make careful, wise choices concerning money and debt. One of the most important passages in scripture regarding this issue of money is God's commandment that every Christian pay their tithes. God sees any decision to withhold tithes and offering from him as completely unacceptable and curse worthy.

So if you are wondering why things are not going well for you, it could be that you are robbing God. And the punishment for robbing God is to live under a curse. You may have a curse in your marriage, finances, health or other area in your life and it is completely related to your decision to keep God's money to yourself.

"Bring the whole tithe into the storehouse, that there may be food in my house. Test me in this," says the Lord Almighty, "and see if I will not throw open the floodgates of heaven and pour out so much blessing that there will not be room enough to store it." (Malachi 3:10)

As the scripture points out, you can only test God when you are in covenant with him. Tithing positions you to establish a covenant with God. So this tithing principle will only work if you are bringing your tithes to God's house. Once you have done your part, then it is God's turn to do his part. And when times get hard, you can put God to the test. And take it from me, God will be true to His Word.

I am a witness that tithing can open doors for those that commit to taking care of His earthly house (the church). This is true in any area that you choose to test God in. If His house is a priority to you, then your house will be a priority to him.

I know that tithing can be difficult. I know that tithing is accompanied by the fear of lack. It was very difficult when I first began tithing as a sophomore in college. It was extremely difficult to see money leave my hand as a full time student working a part time job. But I made a decision to obey the commands of God because I couldn't afford to live under a curse. Even now, 14 years after I began, tithing can sometimes be a difficult decision to make. Especially if I ever miss a Sunday at church and don't have the opportunity to pay that week's tithe. Then the next time I attend service I have to pay the tithe for the week I missed and the tithe for the current week. I have found that to be really painful. Especially because I know that I can do a lot of other things with that money.

But because I have been faithful with taking care of God's house, I have had the opportunity to test God on several occasions. When we moved into our new home and the people who wanted to rent our old home changed their minds at the last minute, I put God to the test. When I was in the hospital about to give birth to my first son and the doctors said they were going to begin preparing me for a C-section, I put God to the test. And when I decided to stop working so I could focus on doing His work full time, I put God to the test. There has never been a time, as a tither, when I tested God, and He didn't do what He was obligated to do. In the case of our home situation, three days after I prayed and put God to the test, we were contacted by a wonderful couple who was interested in purchasing our home. In the case of the C-section, less than 15 minutes after I put God to the test, my beautiful son Jonathan was born by vaginal delivery. And when I tested God about leaving my job to do His work, you can see for yourself the outcome. I was able to write and publish this book.

So when I say that tithing works, trust me, it works.

Bills, Bills, Bills

Another reason to pay your tithes is to help pay the bills of the church. As a person that worships, sends your kids to and participate in activities of the church, if you don't help pay for the electricity, water, or gas that is required to keep the building operational, who will? It is up to the body of Christ to take care of the house they worship in.

But there are a lot of people that don't pay their tithes because they distrust what the pastor or the church will do with the money. But as I see it, I pay my tithe out of obedience to God. I am still in covenant with God and God will still honor that covenant because I have done what He commanded me to do. He simply told me to bring the tithe to his house. What the pastor or church chooses to do with the money is between them and God.

In case you are new to this tithing principle, tithes are equal to 10 percent of your income. So if you earn one hundred dollars, the tithe will be ten dollars; for twenty dollars, the tithe will be two dollars, etc. To calculate your tithes, multiply the amount of money by 0.10. I pay tithes on paychecks (net pay, some people pay the tithe on the gross amount), gifts, tax returns, and any form of income that I bring in.

Once you begin paying your tithes, God is obligated to supply all of your needs in an abundant way. Stop living under the curse in your marital relationship. Make a commitment to paying your tithe, no matter how big or small it may be, and watch God open up the windows of heaven and pour you out a marital blessing that you don't have enough room to receive.

I'll pay for it later

Let me also say a word about credit cards and financing purchases. When you charge something on your credit card or finance a purchase, it means you are taking a product home with the promise to pay for it later. So when you choose not to pay what you owe, you are a thief in God's eyes. It is one thing to have called the creditor to request additional time to make the payment but it is called theft when you have simply chosen not to hold up your end of the bargain. And God will not bless any crime. So if you cannot get out of your money slump, it may be that you are not trustworthy in God's sight and therefore, he is not interested in helping you with your finances.

As a modern day Mrs. 31 you can begin your path of financial security by practicing wisdom and discretion in your spending habits. You and your husband should come up with a budget including a spending, saving and investing plan and ensure that you both follow that plan to the letter. Use coupons, buy 1 get 1 free deals and comparison shop to ensure you use the families' money to purchase things that benefit the family. Teach your children the value of a dollar so they aren't always expecting the highest priced clothes, shoes or latest gadgets. Begin seeing money as a resource that has the ability to run out if not used wisely. Understand that the more money you can preserve and save, the less work you have to do outside of the home to help provide for the family. Conversely, recognize that the longer you delay in becoming financially wise and savvy, the longer your dreams for your family will be delayed.

You can build your house by paying the debt that you owe and by making it your mission to build or maintain your family's credit.

Chapter 12

The Mistress is Physically Attractive

"Her arms are strong for her tasks. She is clothed in fine linen and purple." Proverbs 31:17b and 22b (NIV)

When you picture the mistress, what characteristics about her physical appearance come to mind? You certainly don't think about a haggardly looking woman. Your mind automatically pictures a woman that is well manicured and well dressed so that she is always presentable for her man. The mistress is physically appealing to her man in a way that makes him proud to have her on his arm. She must look this way because she wants to keep his attention on her.

I am sure that what I am about to say is not news to any of you. But just to make sure we are all on the same page, each of us needs to understand that men are visual creatures. When Adam was first introduced to Eve, his initial response was "Whoa!" A man will first be drawn to a woman's physical features before deciding whether or not he wants to get to know more about her. So the way you present yourself is vitally important to your husband.

When you first began dating your husband, you spent hours shopping or going through your entire wardrobe to pick out outfits that he would find attractive. You made sure that your hair and nails were done. You shaved your legs and maintained the space between your legs. You had your eyebrows plucked. You ate better and worked out to keep your jiggling body parts from becoming too excessive.

Well, it's time that you get back into the game.

If you are not already doing so, you must put your appearance back on your priority list. However you looked when you initially attracted him to you is how you're expected to look to keep him attracted to you. Our description of Mrs.31 indicates that she is physically fit and her clothing is made of the best materials. In other words, this wife is well kept.

Mrs. 31 teaches us that it is never okay for a wife to let herself go.

Years ago I heard a comedian say that no man wants to take a woman in public that he has to explain things about. In other words, men want someone they can be proud to have on their arms. They want a woman who has taken the time to dress nicely, applied her makeup well and is sporting nice hands and feet. No matter her size, weight, or height every woman is attractive. It's all about how she presents herself that counts. She can be a size 2 or size 42 and still have sex appeal and be attractive. For each wife, it's about working with what you have and ensuring that you represent yourself and your husband well.

I have to admit that I really struggle in this area. I am all about being comfortable. And heels and dresses are not my idea of comfort. I would normally reserve that type of clothing for a night out on the town. I usually come to bed in whatever is most comfortable, no matter how many holes the material has. I wrap my hair up in whatever way will prevent me from losing sleep and I walk around the house in items that look better on a 4 year old child (like my Spongebob squarepants pajamas) than a wife.

But in my effort to please my husband visually I have to make a conscious effort to step outside of my comfort zone. That is not to say that I can never be comfortable again. That just means that my level of comfort shouldn't be the only thing that I am concerned with. For me, that means fewer instances of wearing tennis shoes and ponytails and more times when I wear more fashionable clothing. It means that even if I choose to wear tennis shoes and ponytails I still present myself as attractive, whatever my husband's definition of attractive is. And this is also what other wives must do as they seek to become their husband's mistress.

It is no different than wanting to see your husband look his best. You don't want to take him out in public when he doesn't have a haircut, wearing old worn clothes and shoes and hasn't bothered to shave in a few days. You want someone you can be proud to have on your arm. You want someone that others would take a second look at (for all of the positive reasons, of course). You don't want someone that you are embarrassed by or ashamed of.

Wives need to develop that same mindset that we had when we were single and trying to catch a man.

Because if we don't take the time to invest in our appearance, we will be single again. When you dress keep your husband's desires and wishes in mind.

Invest in heels. There is nothing sexy about flats. I've talked to a number men and not one of them has said that he preferred flats over a sexy high heel shoe. Now the type and color vary by men's preferences but they all like sexy shoes. Have your man escort you to the shoe store and let him pick out a sexy high heel shoe for you. It will not only turn him on but it will also make you feel sexy or maybe a little naughty. If you absolutely cannot wear them when out on the town with your husband at least wear them in the bedroom. This journey doesn't require you to dress like a lady of the night but may require you to add a few pieces to your wardrobe to spruce it up a little. Your husband is probably tired of seeing you come to bed in sweats and a t-shirt that has turned 8 shades of red. Wear something cute that is comfy. If you and your husband have different ideas on what is attractive or sexy then you need to compromise with him. He may prefer that you wear short, tight fitting clothes which may make you feel as if you are showing too much skin. In that case, compromise by wearing either short or tight fitting clothing but not both at the same time. Or agree to wear it when you two are out on the town but not every time you leave the house. Shop together and let him pick out outfits that he wants to see you wear. If your husband thinks you look hot in red, your wardrobe should have plenty of red pieces. If he prefers long hair, don't cut it short. If he hates to see you in a ponytail, be willing to wear it to his liking on most occasions. Make sure you wear makeup if that is his preference or go bare faced if he prefers the more natural look.

My husband hates when I wear colored nail polish. He prefers the look of a French tip. So when I go to the nail shop I always get the French pedicure.

This is how a wise woman and mistress adapts to her man. She is not haughty or prideful while asserting her independence and her feminist beliefs. She knows what pleases her man and is willing to do whatever necessary to keep her investment secure.

Since men are visual creatures, we must keep in mind that however we normally present ourselves, is the image that will be etched in their minds throughout the day. So always be aware of how you market your product to your husband. No one wants to open an unattractive gift no matter how good the product inside may be. And no one wants to shop in a store that looks unkempt. So there is no reason to think that your man will want to shop in your store when the packaging is unappealing. He may do it out of necessity but wouldn't the experience be better if he did it out of desire? You want your husband to be excited enough to want to open you up (pun intended). So become a billboard or commercial for yourself in an effort to keep your man happy at home.

After Adam saw his wife's beauty he said "This is now bone of my bones and flesh of my flesh" (Genesis

2:23a, NIV). In other words, "This is my woman. She belongs to me." Notice, it wasn't until after he saw how beautiful she was that he claimed her as his own. If a man isn't attracted to his woman, it will show up in his actions. He won't display as much affection for her in front of others. But when he finds her physically attractive, he displays public affection as a way to indicate that she is spoken for. He also does this because he will want to be closer to her.

The bottom line ladies, is that a mistress takes time to invest in her appearance. She realizes that her man wants to see her at her best.

And as a wife, we have to learn to keep our appearances up for the sake of our marriage. I once saw a story on television where a husband began having an affair with another woman. Determined not to lose her man, his wife began dressing attractively and surprising him at his job. When the husband saw his co-workers reactions to how attractive his wife was, the husband stop seeing his mistress and reconciled with his wife.

This story teaches us that a man wants a woman that other men are attracted to. Somehow it makes him feel like he has won the prize and makes him stick his chest out a little further. This story confirmed for me that appearances are very important to men.

So take some time to choose a fashionable outfit that is appropriate to your destination. Play around with different hairstyles and makeup. Play around with different fabrics and clothing. If you lack fashion sense like me, ask a friend who is good at putting pieces together to help you, look in magazines, or find information on the internet on how to coordinate your outfits.

You deserve to look your best and your husband deserves to have you look your best.

Public Image is Important

Proverbs 31:25-6 says Mrs. 31 "is clothed with strength and dignity. In other words, her presence exudes strength and dignity.

In addition to having an attractive spouse, men also want a woman who knows how to act appropriately in public places. Women that are loud, unruly or have no boundaries are often an embarrassment to the men in their lives. A sweet and quiet spirit with a sense of humor is what a lot of men that I've talked to find most attractive about a woman.

"I hate that my wife always has to be the center of attention. When she is loud and boastful I find her behavior embarrassing and disrespectful. I wish that she would turn it off sometimes."

Mrs. 31 has appropriate etiquette when speaking and interacting with others and during meal times. She doesn't have to have the spotlight all of the time. She recognizes that when she steps in public she is a representative of God and her husband. Therefore, she is careful about how she walks, talks and dresses. She is careful about the places she goes, the company she keeps and her actions. She doesn't want to do anything to disrespect or dishonor God, her husband or her family.

Chapter 13

The Mistress is Sexually Available and Sexually Adventurous

Debunking the Myth

Why is sex such a taboo subject among God's people? Why does the church shy away from talking about this vitally important topic and the role it plays in every person's life?

There is no use in hiding it any longer. Christians have sex. And some of us even enjoy it! Now, the secret is out.

So since we now know that everyone, including Christians, have sex, we should feel free about openly discussing it. It is my firm belief that people should be able to go to the church and to the body of Christ to get answers regarding sexual issues. If people cannot come to the church to get answers for real life questions, where are they supposed to go? And as the body of Christ and as God's representatives here on earth, when people approach us and want to discuss sex, we need to stop shying away from the subject and offer practical advice based on God's word.

After all, sex was God's idea.

So to view sex as anything other than holy and sacred is

a mistake. It is one of the many things that our bodies were created to do. And since almost every adult will have some form of sexual experience in his/her lifetime it's time to stop dodging this subject of sex and begin giving people the freedom to feel comfortable with it.

The Bible says that "everything that God created is good" (1 Timothy 4:4) and sex is one of those things. Sex is supposed to create an impenetrable bond between a man and his wife. It is supposed to be pleasurable. It is supposed to be fun. It is supposed to be enjoyed and should not be considered a chore or duty. Sex is a beautiful gift given to you by your Creator to enjoy within the confines of your marital relationship. It is no coincidence that your husband's male parts are the exact opposite of and fit perfectly with your female parts. God did that intentionally so that each spouse would bring something different, special, and unique to the marriage bed. Consider it your wedding gift from God. He was present during the ceremony and He came bearing this wonderful gift for you to enjoy for the rest of your married life.

God sees sex between a husband and wife as holy and scared and His word encourages an active sex life (1 Corinthians 7:5). If you have been told otherwise, you have been lied to. So instead of seeing sex as a burden, as immoral or unholy, begin seeing it as God's perfect gift to you that comes along with having the title 'wife.'

Being bad in the bedroom

How would your husband describe you in the bedroom? Would he use words like lazy, inhibited, and disinterested? What about boring, lifeless or predictable? If your husband uses any of these or similar words to describe you in the bedroom, then girlfriend, we have a serious problem. And that problem will likely result in an unfulfilling sex life and/or marital relationship. We don't serve a boring, lifeless or predictable God and since we were created in His image (Genesis 1:26) we were not created to exhibit these traits in any area of our lives.

If sex was supposed to be strictly a routine, non-stimulating act that didn't involve any type of pleasure, then God's plan to have us be fruitful and multiply would be flawed. No one would seek sex from their spouse if the only benefit was to procreate. With children, comes responsibility, work, financial obligations and less free time. Having children isn't a big enough motivator. Therefore, sex had to be designed to do more than just allow us to procreate and replenish the earth. Sex feels good because God created sex to serve many purposes. Sex was not only meant to produce children, it was also to be used to comfort, bring closeness and to bring pleasure in the marriage.

Hebrews 13:4a (NIV) says "Marriage is honorable among all, and the bed undefiled". Do you see that ladies? A relationship between a man and his wife is something that God sees as worthy of honor. And a very important part of that marital relationship is sex. The verse goes on to say that the marriage bed is undefiled. Defiled means [11]"To make filthy or dirty". Having a sexual relationship with your husband is not dirty, filthy or immoral. If it was, would God have created it? Absolutely not! There is nothing dirty, filthy or immoral about God so He is incapable of creating anything with those characteristics. So when the bible says that the marriage bed is undefiled that means that the marriage bed is not a place that is considered dirty, filthy or immoral in God's eyes.

Therefore, as long as you both are agreeable and the sexual encounter only involves the two of you, God deems any sexual act between a husband and wife as acceptable. That means where you choose to lay with your husband is completely up to you and your husband. It also means that

Toys are okay.

Different positions are okay.

Different non-public places are okay.

Several times a day is okay.

Having sex during the day is okay.

Having sex during your menstrual cycle is okay (but it can get messy.)

It's okay to be on top.

It's okay to be in front of.

It's okay to be on the floor.

It's okay to be outside of the bedroom.

It's okay to be sitting.

It's okay to be standing.

It's okay to be kneeling.

Oral sex is okay.

Being bad in the bedroom (or in the car, on the floor, in the dining room, or where ever you choose to give your love to your spouse) is totally okay with God.

2 things that are not okay with God

1. Different partners are NOT okay. That is because being with someone other than the person you are legally married to is a sin.

2. Pornography is NOT Okay. Viewing porn isn't okay because you are watching something that is supposed to be sacred between a husband and wife for your own lustful pleasure which makes it a sin. Now I know that there are hundreds of thousands of men that like to watch porn. Some are even addicted to it. But as I said before, it is not your job to be God. Tell your husband your thoughts and feelings about it. Let him know what you believe to be God's stance on it. Urge him to stop viewing it and instead participate in a session of porn with you. But after you have done all of these things,

the only thing you should do is pray. Pray that God will deliver him from the grips of porn. Pray that God will put such a sour taste in his mouth that every time he even thinks about looking at it, he get nauseous. Understand that porn is very addictive and even if he has the desire to stop viewing it, completely letting it go will be difficult for him. It doesn't mean that he doesn't love you. It doesn't mean that he is not attracted to you. His desire to watch porn is not necessarily an indicator that he is dissatisfied sexually with you. It's just something that he picked up along the way and since he is a visual person, he gets stimulated by visually pleasing things. He probably began viewing pornography in his early teens, prior to ever meeting you. For men, they are really visual and really sexual so when both of those elements are combined, it makes sense why so many men like to view pornography. Your job is to seek God for change.

Lessons from a Married Mistress

King Solomon is the author of the book of Proverbs, the same book where our description of Mrs.31 is found. According to the bible, King Solomon was the wisest person to have ever walked this earth. And although he was very wise, King Solomon also had a weakness for women. As mentioned earlier 1 Kings 11:3 says that King Solomon had 700 wives, princesses and 300 concubines (girlfriends).

What I find fascinating is that of all of the women that the wise King had in his life, he wrote a book about only one of them, his bride Shulamith. The title of that book is The Song of Solomon. That also caught my attention. His other books had regular titles like Proverbs and Ecclesiastes. But the book the described his marital relationship with his wife is named *The Song of Solomon*. That indicates that Shulamith had the king singing!

Let's take a closer look to see how this one woman was able to stand out from the other 999 women that King Solomon had in his life.

In Song of Solomon 7:7-9 (NIV) Solomon says to Shulamith "Your stature is like that of the palm, and your breasts like clusters of fruit. I said, "I will climb the palm tree; I will take hold of its fruit." May your breasts be like clusters of grapes on the vine, the fragrance of your breath like apples, and your mouth like the best wine. Shulamith's response to her husband in verses 11-12 is "Come, my beloved, let us go to the countryside, let us spend the night in the villages. Let us go early to the vineyards to see if the vines have budded, if their blossoms have opened, and if the pomegranates are in bloom— there I will give you my love".

In plain terms, Solomon told his wife that he couldn't wait to climb up her body (which he described as a palm tree) and get his hands on her breasts (which he described as clusters of fruit). He said he wanted to take hold of her breasts as if they were grapes on a vine and he wanted to experience her savory kiss.

Shulamith responded by proposing that she and her husband get away for the night, rise up early and make love. She told him that he would be able to see for himself if her (grape) vines had budded i.e. if her breast nipples were erect; a sign that indicates that a woman is sexually aroused.

What we are witnessing is that Solomon is sexually attracted to his wife and fanning the flames of passion with her by describing what he would like to do with her sexually. And Shulamith is fully engaged, cooperative and openly receptive to her husband's flirting.

There are 3 important lessons that Shulamith teaches married women.

Lesson #1: Flirt with your husband

Flirting can be fun and outrageously seductive. Flirting is often the first tool that a mistress will use with her lover to build his anticipation of what to expect later. Shulamith doesn't shy away from her husband's sexually suggestive words. She embraces them and even flirts back with a few sexually suggestive words of her own. So flirting with her husband should not make any wife feel awkward, shy or intimidated. Flirting should make you feel naughty. Flirting should get your sexual juices flowing. And flirting should make you feel powerful as you observe the effect that it is has on your husband.

Below are some ideas about specific ways you can flirt with your man.

Share your sexual fantasies with him and try to create his. Describe in explicit detail all of the sexual things you want to do to pleasure him. Describe in very specific detail what you would like him to do to you sexually. Fondle him underneath the dinner table. Write a note on a napkin detailing the many ways you want to please him sexually and pass it to him while he is in the middle of eating dinner. Watch how quickly he rushes through his meal! Try leaving sexy notes in his car, in his briefcase and/or in his coat pocket promising him an unforgettable evening. Use sexting (text messaging sexy messages) as a way to flirt. Take a pole dancing class and show your husband your moves. Perform a strip tease for him. Talk dirty while he penetrates you. Let him know how much he is pleasing you at that moment. A man needs to know that he can please his woman sexually. He also needs to know that you desire to have sex with him. It makes him feel adequate. So whenever you get the chance to tell him how much you enjoy having sex with him, take it.

For some women, flirting will come easily and naturally. But for others, flirting takes practice. If you are one of those women that don't feel comfortable engaging in flirtatious behavior or saying sexually suggestive words to your husband, then you need to learn to get comfortable. It's time to bring out a new bag of treats to offer your man. Don't worry about feeling silly or worry that your husband will laugh at you. Believe me, if you say the right words and engage in the right behaviors that get his attention, he won't think that you are silly or funny. That grin that you will see on his face won't be because he wants to laugh at you but it will be a smile of satisfaction. Don't be ashamed to practice in front of a mirror if you need to. You can also write down the words that you want to say and practice saying them before attempting to use them with your husband.

Lesson #2: Be sexually available for your husband

Shulamith didn't make any excuses about why she didn't want to have sex. In fact, in the passage above, she didn't express any reservations or hesitation with what her husband was proposing to do with her sexually. She made herself available to please her man. What Shulamith teaches wives is to be open to your husband's advances.

Rejection damages relationships.

Can you imagine a mistress turning down her man's request for sex? It is unfathomable and sounds so UN-mistress like. To think she would have the nerve to reject her lover and still be able to get what she needs from him is crazy. A mistress has enough wisdom to realize that one of a man's most important needs is sexual gratification. Therefore, for her, rejection is never an option.

Rejection hurts a man's pride and causes damage to a relationship. And frequent rejection will make him question his adequacy as a lover. It is not biblical to reject your husband's sexual advances. So stop rejecting him and blowing him off. The only time you should turn your husband down is if you both agree to do something at another, more convenient time. No one, including you, likes to feel the sting of rejection so there is no reason to do this to your husband.

Why you shouldn't say No

Even well intentioned good guys can fall into temptation. So one of the main reasons that it's not okay to reject your husband's attempts to have sex with you is because you never know how close he will come to going outside of the marital bed for sexual gratification.

He may already be struggling to remain faithful. He may be going through a tough time emotionally and need to feel connected to someone. He may be at a point in his life where he is questioning his adequacy or attractiveness. So you should never reject his attempts to be intimate with you.

Satan will always test people in areas where they are the weakest. He offered Jesus bread after Jesus had fasted for 40 days because that is the area where Jesus was the weakest at that time in his life. So if you reject your husband sexually you should expect that he will be presented with a temptation in that area.

And don't be naïve enough to think that your Christian man won't stray. You are delusional if you think that your hubby can't or won't be tempted by another woman after not getting his needs met at home.

Another reason not to reject sex with your husband is because sex is God's gift to your husband for marrying you. So to keep a gift to yourself when it was intended to give to someone else is called theft. And all crime must be punished which may be the reason for your marital discord.

Change your strategy

Have you ever noticed that as soon as you inform your current electric, cable or phone provider that you are going to switch your services to their competitor, they offer you the best deals in order to retain you? But none of them ever call and offer you anything of benefit to you until you are ready to leave them. My question is, why do you have to threaten to leave before they offer you their best deal?

I have noticed that in most cases, wives don't begin fighting for their marriages until another woman enters the picture and threatens to take their husbands away from them. Then, their husbands become special. Then their husbands become a priority. But we wives must learn to be proactive instead of being reactive.

Companies also frequently change their marketing strategies because they want to keep their customers interested. They market in different ways to grab and keep their customers coming back to shop at their stores. They have meetings to pitch ideas and to evaluate what changes need to be made to please the consumer. If they find out that their competitor is offering a better deal, they change their game plan and their marketing strategy to keep their loyal customers from switching sides. These are the exact same steps we need to take as wives to keep our husbands interested in us. The status quo simply won't do. We need to continue to fight to keep our marriages intact from day one because once our husbands find out there are better deals elsewhere it will be harder to convince them to stay committed to us.

You must step up to the plate and take your swing at keeping the home fires burning. DO NOT continue to make excuses to your husband about your lack of interest in sex, your lack of enthusiasm about sex or your unwillingness to have sex on a regular basis. As understanding as your husband may be, soon his physical needs will become paramount which may lead him to seek a relationship outside of the marriage. And although your husband is responsible for his own actions, if you are withholding sex, love or intimacy, you will also bear some of the responsibility for any infidelity.

If you are on your menstrual cycle, then take the time to find other exciting ways to please your man. If you are tired, give him a quickie. If you have a headache, take an aspirin and get a nap before he gets home so you are ready to receive him. If there is an issue of a low sex drive, then seek help from a medical professional. If you are unhappy or uncomfortable with your body, then go to the gym. If you are okay with what you see in the mirror, then use what you have and work your magic on your man.

I have heard many men say that there is nothing more attractive than a self confident woman-and that includes being confident in the bedroom. You cannot fully enjoy yourself with your husband if you are concentrating on how large your stomach is, how much your thighs are jiggling or how flat your bottom is. None of that matters to your husband especially when he wants to have sex. He married you with that flat bottom and he has chosen to stay married to you with that large stomach and jiggling thighs of yours. So get over your imperfections when you are having sexual relations with your husband. Take the time to workout, eat right and drink plenty of water during the day until you get the body shape you desire. But in the meantime, don't deprive yourself or your husband of a great sex life while you are waiting on your body to change shape. Your man should not have to wait until you lose weight to have sex. While he is waiting, another woman who is shaped worse than you may come along and offer your husband a bite of her apple that he may not be able to resist.

Also, stop being so temperamental and moody. That is a complete turn off and eventually your husband will not want to deal with you. He will seek out companionship with someone that is easier to get along with.

Marriage is supposed to be fun. It's supposed to be a safe environment where a husband and wife are totally unashamed with each other. It's supposed to be where you can let your hair down and be comfortable being exactly who God created you to be. There shouldn't be rules or stipulations in the relationship that determine if he will be allowed to have sex. Your man should not have to wait until you are in the mood to have sex. And your man shouldn't have to wait until you stop being mad at him to have sex.

Lesson #3: Be sexually adventurous with your husband

To be a mistress, you must not only be sexually available for your husband but you must also be sexually adventurous with your husband. There is no way around it. It is a requirement for having a fulfilling sex life. Sex and all of the activities leading up to sex is when the mistress is in her comfort zone. Sex is the secret weapon that a mistress has. This is not an area where she is shy, inhibited, disinterested or uninvolved. Sex is the area where she excels. Even if she can't get things right outside of the bedroom, she does whatever necessary to get things right inside of the bedroom.

It was Shulamith's idea to get away for the night. And it was her idea to make love in a new place.

Shulamith is the type of a mistress that all wives should aspire to become.

Let's face it. Without good sex, there are very few people that will be pleased with their marriages. I have found this to be true regardless of how great of a cook, mother, companion or wife a woman is. Women are supposed to enjoy sex just as much as men do. Enjoying sex doesn't make you less of a Christian. In fact, trying new things with your husband makes you a wise wife. God intended marriages to last a life time and sex is a huge part of the marital relationship. God created sex to be a pleasurable experience for both spouses so that both would stay interested in the relationship.

Sex was intended to allow us to feel closer to our husbands and to keep each spouse faithful to one another. So one of the most important things you can do towards becoming your husband's mistress is to get rid of your inhibitions about sex. Let your husband love you in a new way, in a new place and in a new position. Relax your ideas about what you think you know, ideas that you have been taught by your family and friends, etc if they don't line up with the word of God. Your hang-ups will interfere with your marriage and sex life if you don't change your old ways of thinking. God's word doesn't have any restrictions on marital sex. You and your husband are free to choose how often, where or when you should engage in sexual activities. God has given you permission to have yourself a good time. You must be open to exploring new things in order to keep things interesting and spicy. Your husband doesn't want spaghetti every Tuesday served on the same dish at the same time in the same location for the rest of his life. That is boring and predictable. Your sex life should add some flavor to your relationship and should be anything but boring and predictable.

[12]"Make your time together unforgettable. This means the fun, non-committal things such as mind-blowing intimacy, indulgent fantasies, and listening when he needs to talk. These are the things he wants from you. Be his fantasy girl. He has enough reality in his life."

And as soon as you accept that sex is meant to be enjoyed, explored, and appreciated, the sooner you will experience sexual freedom.

I am going to teach you a new way to think about sex.

Whenever you hear the word sex, I want your mind to automatically remember that SEX stands for Sensuous Encounters that are X-Rated.

Let's take a closer look at our new acronym.

1. S- Sensuous is defined as "being alive to the

pleasure to be received through the 5 senses".

Let's dissect the definition.

Being alive-simply means not to be dead. Deadness includes laying there waiting to get it over with, being uninvolved during the act of love making, not being present and in the moment or simply not enjoying having sex.

Pleasure-what feels good, what's enjoyable

To be received-incoming, what is being given to each person

The 5 senses-sight, smell, taste, hear, and touch

So the definition of sensuous is to be lively and enjoy what feels good to you based on what you receive through sight, smell, taste, hearing and touching.

To make it more plain, sensuous means, being a full participant and enjoying yourself when you are having sex with your husband. Enjoy what you see, what you smell, what you taste, what you hear and what you touch.

2. E-Encounters simply means a meeting that was planned or unplanned, expected or unexpected, brief or long, between 2 people

3. X-X-rated means being as bad as you wanna be.

And your challenge is to think S.E.X.

S.E.X. gives you permission to stop holding yourself back. You can now release what you have been holding onto. Allow yourself to explore, enjoy and be excited. Stop being so timid, shy, boring, uninterested and uninvolved when you are with your husband.

Creativity is Sexy

There are too many accessories and ideas on the market for your sex life to be boring.

Aren't the best gifts the kind that have multiple functions?

Everyone prefers a remote control that turns on the TV, the DVD player, the fan, the lights and anything else in the household. Or what about a car? Everyone prefers a car with all of the bells and whistles with automatic gears, windows that go up or down with the touch of a button, and other features that you cannot find in a base model. A base model is functional but boring. It will do the job but you won't enjoy the ride nearly as much.

Not to compare you to a remote control or a car, but the point is that everyone prefers the deluxe model as opposed to a basic model. Wives need to learn to become the deluxe model in their marriages. A deluxe model wife is daring and bold, flirtatious, spontaneous, and likes to have fun. If you don't have a clue as to how to flirt or what to do to have fun in the bedroom, you can find those answers on the internet, in a book, or by asking your husband. There is no excuse for not knowing because there are too many resources available to help you.

And while you are learning ways to spice up your sex life, don't forget to incorporate elements of surprise. Dress up and role play. Ask him for a quickie as soon as he comes home. Join him in the shower and focus on pleasuring him. Plan a hotel getaway. Decorate the room, have a delicious meal and let him be the dessert. Indulge. You can include massages using warm oil by candle light, use relaxing music that sets the mood for the evening, try a bubble bath or steamy shower and take turns lathering each other up, try a new technique while in the water. I guarantee that the mistress isn't boring or inhibited in the bedroom because she wants to keep her man permanently. So she is pulling out all of the stops.

Your job is to find your adventurous side. Surprise him by suggesting a new position in a new location. Be spontaneous. Be passionate. Enjoy the gift that God has given you. Take pleasure in the giving and the receiving of the gift. Learn to appreciate and enjoy your gift. Fill your husband and let him fill you. Stop holding back in the bedroom.

Oral Sex

Ok ladies. Originally I was going to include specific things that can be done to please your husband orally (all based on scientific research of course). But as I began to research ideas on the internet, all of the information that I found was a little too hot for this book. So instead of spelling everything out, I've decided to give you a few tips and resources where you can find all of the information yourself.

Giving

When giving oral sex, one of the most important things to remember is that men like to watch you perform. So whatever position you are in make sure that your husband can see what is going on below his bellybutton. Another thing to remember is the more you enjoy it, the more he will enjoy it. If oral pleasure is something that your husband has been asking for, that means that it is high on his sex priority list. So you better get over your hang ups about it. If giving oral pleasure to your husband is not something that you are interested in doing, just remember that there are other women who are interested in doing it for you.

Sometimes it's just nice to surprise your hubby. Try doing it when he least expects it. It can be a good way to wake him up in the morning or a way to greet him when he gets home from work. I won't go into more detail. You all get the point. If you want more information about this subject, I found an author by the name of Jack Hutson that you can look up on the internet. His website offers tips on positions, attitude, foreplay, etc. But be warned, he is not a Christian author so if you are sensitive to certain words (there aren't any pictures on his site), this may not be the site for you. I have included the website under the resource section at the end of the book.

Receiving

Some thoughts of science say that a woman's clitoris has more nerve endings than any other part of the human body. That means that for most women, the clitoris serves as the primary pleasure zone and is the main factor in achieving orgasm. In fact, for a large percentage of women, direct stimulation of the clitoris is the only way they can achieve orgasm. It's a woman's job to show her man how to please her. So as a woman you need to be comfortable with your own body. You need to know what brings you pleasure and teach your husband to focus on those areas. You need to be comfortable communicating your sexual needs and desires to your husband and ask for what you want in the bedroom. You must learn how to receive pleasure. And you must learn to be a passionate lover.

Be Passionate

Okay, I know what I'm about to say will offend some of you and make it seem like I'm not much of a Christian. But I am very comfortable and confident in my relationship with God so I'm going to say it anyway because wives must learn to become passionate lovers. When you are with your husband sexually, try to think and act like a porn star sometimes. Even if you have never personally viewed pornography (and I am not promoting the viewing of pornographic materials) you can guess at what types of behaviors are exhibited by those females. Ask yourself the following questions:

How would a woman in a porn film please her man?

How would she attempt to seduce him?

How would she attempt to turn him on sexually?

How would she attempt to please him orally?

How would she attempt to capture his attention outside of the bedroom?

What would she wear?

What would she say?

How would she act?

Then think about your husband's personal preferences. Of all of the answers you came up with to the above questions, which would fit into your marriage? Which would minister to your husband in the bedroom? And I use the word minister because I hope by now that you have learned that your marriage is your ministry. It is a sacred covenant and relationship ordained by God to demonstrate to the world what love, compassion, faith, mercy, forgiveness and grace look like in action. That is why God hates divorce.

It's your husband, it's your marriage. Remind yourself that you are a mistress which means there is nothing off limits with your husband. A Mistress goes above and beyond when it comes to pleasing her man and being pleased by him. Nothing is too naughty or kinky. Being creative is ok. Wake him up to sex, greet him at the door with sex, join him in the shower for a steamy sexual encounter. It's ok to spoil him-get him so spoiled that he has no desire to look elsewhere for sexual gratification.

I suggest trying one new thing, whether it's a new location, new position, new toy, at least 2-3x per month. If you aren't shy and are comfortable with your sexuality then take it up a notch and do it more often than that.

Also, stay in conversations with God and with your husband in an effort to gain knowledge. We have too much on the line and too much at stake to be lax in this area.

As said earlier, marriage is honorable and the marriage bed is undefiled. So to have an inactive, inconsistent, or boring sex life is a disservice to both you and your husband. It's similar to being in bed with a severe cold and refusing to take medicine meant to help you feel better. There may be many medications on the store shelves but if you refuse to take any of them, you will not begin to get well. And the same is true of marriage and sexual relationships within marriages. There are many resources available to teach you what you don't know about sex. So it doesn't make sense to stay uninformed about ways to turn up the heat in your bedroom. Don't just lie in your cold, lifeless, boring marital bed when you have every opportunity to spice things up. A good sex life may not be a priority for you but it is a priority for your man. So if you have the mindset that you can do without sex or you only have sex for your husband's sake, you can prepare yourself for the eventual disintegration of your marriage.

Closing Remarks

I know that your feminist ideologies are screaming at you to resist what you are being encouraged to do. But you cannot work against your husband and expect him to give you his best. And you cannot work against what God has asked of you and expect to experience fulfillment. You are not being asked to become less independent. You are not being asked to get rid of your designer clothes in exchange for a servants outfit. You are only being asked to help your husband in any way you can to become his best self. You are supposed to be there to help him reach his goals. You are supposed to be there to help him get closer to God. If you don't do it, then who will? So if you won't help him grow spiritually, emotionally, mentally or financially, then he doesn't really need you in his life. You are doing these things to give your children a father that is a good role model. You are doing these things so you can have a great marriage. It is absolutely worth all of the effort that you put into it. So don't let your beliefs about independency dissuade you from becoming your husband's mistress.

I know that being married is the hardest challenge you have ever faced. I know that the decisions he makes get underneath your skin. I know that you can barely stand to look at him sometimes. But that is why having God as the foundation of your relationship is so vitally important. That is why you must build your relationship upon the Rock. He is the creator of marriage meaning he knows how it's supposed to work so he is the one you need to go to in order to vent, ask questions and seek help.

The fact that you are reading this book says to me that you are at least open to doing something new. It says to me that deep down you still want to be married to your husband. Otherwise you would not have even bothered picking this book up. So you are not as ready to walk away as you have said. There is still a part of you that has some fight left. So go ahead. Reject all feelings of fear that you may have. Jump right in with both feet and say yes to God's leading.

Even if you are skeptical about this process, what do you have to lose at this point? You can leave and experience the pain of divorce, you can stay and experience the pain of not leaving or you can change how you interact with and treat your husband in an effort to experience some marital satisfaction. Don't walk away before you have done absolutely everything you can do to save your relationship.

I never thought that my relationship with my husband would ever recover from the years of hurt, disappointments, and frustrations in our relationship. Remember, I was filling out divorce papers and had a separate bank account and shopping for apartments when I began my journey. But when I began this journey of becoming a mistress my attitude towards and feelings about my husband began changing for the better. I believe that things changed because I was open to God's intervention in my heart, mind and spirit. I allowed myself to love my husband instead of holding on to the bitterness and anger I felt towards him. And I am a witness that love, passion, desire and respect can be restored if you are open to receiving it into the life of your marriage. I can truly say that the love for my husband has been restored. The attraction for my husband has been restored. The desire to be around my husband has been restored. And the desire to be his wife and to be my best for him has been restored. Yes, I have been challenged. Yes, I have questioned if it was worth all of this effort. Yes, I have faced resistance from my husband at times. Yes, I have had my feelings hurt along the way. But this was something that I needed to do for God, for my children and for myself, it wasn't just about my husband. He just happened to be the recipient of my efforts.

What better way to help wives who are having a difficult time in their marriages than to send someone who was ready to give up herself to let you know that there is hope and redemption available? God had me write this book because there are a lot of women that are struggling in their marriages but don't talk about their struggles or seek the right help. They are embarrassed or think they will be judged for not being able to keep their men happy so they suffer in silence. God knew that I was brave enough to talk openly about my own marital issues so he sent me to give you this information at this very time in your life. Now what will you do with it?

More Lessons

Other lessons on marriage that I wanted to include without writing a whole chapter on each are:

Recognize that your husband wants the same thing that you want from your marriage: to be heard, to be respected, to be appreciated, to be affirmed and to be loved. You will only get from your relationship what you put into the relationship. It's the law of nature. If you put it out in the universe, you should expect that it will come back to you.

Assume Nothing. Don't make assumptions about your husband's thoughts, ideas, words, actions or intentions. Making assumptions will cause a whole lot of stress and strife in the relationship and will create distance in the marriage. If you have a question, ask it directly. And accept his answer as his truth. It doesn't matter whether or not you believe his answer. That is the answer that he has given you at that time. If you need clarity, wisdom or truth, seek God's help.

Fight fair. You don't have to win every argument. You don't always have to go for the win. You don't have to have the last word. Don't do any name calling or hurl insults. When arguing with your husband, don't demean or damage your husband's heart or his character.

Be careful not to become resentful during this process because he is the primary focus. Believe me, if you're meeting his needs, he will gladly meet your needs.

Accept your husband as he is today. Not for what you imagined him to become. But for the man he is right now. And for those stubborn areas in your mate's life that refuse to grow up, you need to fast, pray and support him until those changes take place.

Let go of the need to control every situation and every person. When he gets a day off he may want to hang out with his friends, watch TV or do nothing at all and you need to be okay with that. He gets to define what activities relax him, you don't. Now that doesn't mean that he should never spend time with you or with the children but that just means that you need to give him some freedom to choose how he will spend his free time.

Be okay with being kept out of the details sometimes. You don't have to know everything about every situation all of the time. Sometimes it's good for you to be unaware so others can't add any more items to your to do list.

Be a wife of great moral character. He needs to be able to trust your motives, heart, faithfulness and commitment to him and the family you both have created. He needs to be able to trust you with his deepest fears and most hurtful wounds and know that you won't betray that trust. He needs to know that you will never use the things he has told you against him. You also need to be dependable and reliable.

You have to stand by your man no matter what challenges come up. You have to be emotionally stable and not falter just because something has gone wrong. Your husband needs to know that you will be by his side even if the bottom falls out. If the house gets foreclosed on, if he loses his job or his health, if his relationship with God is not where it should be, he needs to know that you will be with him through any difficult situation.

Married couples talk about kids, marriage, finances and problems. When people get married, their world gets smaller. With a mistress, there is no place for these mundane conversations. They don't talk about the same things; there are a variety of topics to discuss. So find new interests that make for good conversation.

Whenever feelings of doubt or insecurity arise, begin repeating 1 Timothy 4:4 which says "everything that God created is good." And everything includes your husband, your life, and sex.

Take care of your man's needs. Don't say that I'm not doing a job that his momma should've done. If he asks you to do something, run an errand or make yourself available for a certain event, then do it! Stop complaining, talking back and making excuses.

Become the Mistress of the House: managing your time wisely, ensuring the needs of the household are met, bring structure into the home, make your home a safe haven, delegate chores so you have time for yourself and your husband, etc.

Create a relaxing, intimate space for the two of you to

enjoy. Your bedroom has to be treated as scared. It cannot be your dumping ground for toys, mail, diapers, etc. It should appeal to your husband's 5 senses: appealing to the sight by being beautifully and tastefully decorated, clean, organized and de-cluttered; Appealing to smell-not overpowering fragrances but mildly scented candles or incense or just a fresh clean aroma. Appeal to touch-sheets should be comfortable to your husband whether crisp, soft, cotton, silk whatever he finds appealing. Appealing to tastes-nice candies by the bedside, edible accessories like underwear, lotions, powder, etc. Appealing to sound-nice, relaxing or romantic sounds-nature, waterfalls, or whatever appeals.

Designate a "no responsibility night". This is a night where he doesn't have to be responsible –for homework, cleaning, coming straight home after work. Both of you should have a no responsibility night. He has to be responsible all week long so by giving him this time off he can rejuvenate and prepare for the rest of the week.

Relax when it comes to sex. Take your time, explore, get creative and find out what you enjoy. Waiting to get it over with or treating it like a chore or duty is a sure way to push your man into the arms of another woman. There are always women that are willing to do what a wife refuses to do. But this is not their show, not their relationship and not their man. You are the woman wearing his ring. You are the woman with the power, and you are the one with the influence. And you will not allow your inability or unwillingness to enjoy sexual intimacy with your husband ruin your relationship. Do whatever you need to do to get past your sexual hang ups and issues as quickly as possible before it ruins your marriage. Time is not on your side when it comes to ensuring that you are pleasing your husband sexually.

The mistress understands the importance of making her man feel like he is the most admired man on the planet. She recognizes that the support, affirmation and admiration that she gives him is what draws him to a relationship with her. There is no woman on earth that is able to make him feel more worthy, adequate and special than she does. She makes it her mission to ensure that he knows that there is no other man in this world that can fulfill her needs better than he can.

A mistress makes her man feel like superman. She makes him feel like he is worthy and adequate. Your husband should feel invincible while he's married to you. So adore him without reservations, encourage him without wavering and love him without conditions.

You will never be fulfilled in your relationship until you fulfill your obligation to him. You cannot afford to wait until he gets his act together before you decide to become a willing participant in your marriage. You have too much at stake.

The bible says that a man that finds a wife finds a good thing. Don't make your husband doubt God's word by being anything but good to him. Make him feel like he made a good choice by marrying you. Make it your mission to show him why he made a good choice in picking you to be his life partner.

Study Guide Questions

1. What are 3 new things about your husband, about God or about yourself that you have learned by reading this book?

_____

_____

_____

2. What area of your life has your husband asked you to change in order to be the woman of his dreams?

_____

_____

3. Do you want to be your husband's mistress? Why or Why Not?

_____

_____

4. What do you think the scripture found in Matthew 7:1-5 means and how does it apply to your marital relationship?

_____

_____

5. What do you think a mistress would do if her man was losing interest in their relationship?

_____

_____

6. What are you willing to do to ensure you do your

part to have a mutually satisfying relationship with your husband?

_____

_____

7. What type of mistress(es) do you find to be the most challenging for you to become i.e. The Respectful Mistress, The Sexually Adventurous Mistress, etc? Why? What can you do to overcome those challenges?

_____

_____

8. I have been very transparent about the type of wife that I was towards my husband. What do you need to admit about yourself about the role that you have played regarding the state of your relationship with your husband?

_____

_____

9. What are 2 things that you can do immediately in an effort to become your husband's mistress?

_____

_____

10. How can you demonstrate agape love towards your husband?

_____

_____

11. How can you demonstrate unconditional respect towards your husband?

_____

_____

12. In what areas of his life does your husband need encouragement?

_____

_____

13. Read Proverbs 12:4. What does this passage mean? In what ways does this verse apply to your actions towards your husband?

_____

_____

14. Based on what you read, what power/influence does a mistress have?

_____

_____

15. How do you think your husband will respond once you begin implementing your new role as a mistress?

_____

_____

16. What do you think it will take to become your husband's mistress?

_____

17. What areas in your relationship need to be healed? What do you need to do as a first step towards the healing process?

_____

_____

18. Which mistress are you excited about exploring and introducing your husband to? Why?

_____

_____

19. Which mistress can you become today? Why did you choose her?

_____

_____

20. In the Stripping 101 section you learned the importance of ensuring that the experiences you bring into your marriage are in line with your objective for your marriage.

Your assignment is to write a resume based on how you have performed as a wife. I want you to detail the positive and negative traits you have brought to your marriage.

Wife Resume

Objective....To have a successful marriage

Past experiences

Title: Wife

When my husband and I argue, I usually

_____

(curse, shut down, disrespect him, go for the win, listen attentively, etc).

Write a few sentences about a past argument with your husband. Briefly describe the following:

What happened?

_____

_____

How did you react?

_____

The end result?

_____

When my husband does something that hurts or offends me, I usually

_____

(get depressed, seek revenge, belittle or criticize him)

Write a few sentences about a time when you were hurt

or offended by your husband. Briefly describe the following:

What happened?

_____

_____

How did you react?

_____

The end result?

_____

When I feel unloved by my husband, I usually

_____

(withdraw, seek love elsewhere, talk to my husband about how I feel).

Write a few sentences about a time when your husband made you feel unloved. Briefly describe the following:

What happened?

_____

_____

How did you react?

_____

The end result?

_____

Now that you have learned how to become your

husband's mistress, write a resume detailing how you will respond to future challenges in your marriage.

Mistress Resume

Objective....To have a successful, mutually fulfilling marriage.

Future experiences

Title: Mistress

When my husband and I argue, I will

a._____

b._____

c._____

If my husband does something that hurts or offends me, I will

a._____

b._____

c._____

When I feel unloved by my husband, I will

a._____

b._____

c._____

The 30 Day Married Mistress Challenge

I'm sure you've heard the saying that it takes 30 days to make or break a habit. This book is designed to help each of us take a single step everyday on a journey towards a fantastic marital relationship.

You can do any of these in any order. Keep track of your husband's response when you try one of these new things. That way you will know what he likes and what captures his attention.

1. Wake him up to sex

Husband's response: little response   he liked it   he loved it

2. Email/text words of encouragement

Husband's response: little response   he liked it   he loved it

3. Present him with a list of 10 reasons why you fell in love with him

   Husband's response: little response   he liked it   he loved it

4. Do something nice for him with a card that says "just because"

  Husband's response: little response   he liked it   he loved it

5. Write him a letter committing to be the woman of his dreams. Be specific in detailing what he can expect to see from you from this point forward

Husband's response: little response   he liked it   he loved it

6. Tell him why you respect/admire him at least 2 times today

Husband's response: little response   he liked it   he loved it

7. Have some fun-go to a movie or out dancing or just sit and enjoy each other's company

  Husband's response: little response   he liked it   he loved it

8. Ask him about his dreams/desires. Next ask him how you can help him achieve these things

Husband's response: little response   he liked it   he loved it

9. Leave him a note promising him a wild night to remember and follow through on your promise

Husband's response: little response   he liked it   he loved it

10. Invite him to take a shower or soak in a tub with you. Set the mood

Husband's response: little response   he liked it   he loved it

11. Make his favorite meal

Husband's response: little response   he liked it   he loved it

12. Watch a sports event or movie of his choice and remain "present"-don't be mentally checked out. Have the kids in their rooms and prepare snacks for them so they don't interrupt your time together.

Husband's response: little response   he liked it   he loved it

13. Wake him up to oral pleasure

Husband's response: little response   he liked it   he loved it

14. Allow him time away with his friends without complaining or rushing him to come home

Husband's response: little response   he liked it   he loved it

15. Ask him how you can please him

Husband's response: little response   he liked it   he loved it

16. Implement 1 way to please him-wear heels, cut your hair, begin dieting

Husband's response: little response   he liked it   he loved it

17. Go to a sports bar or favorite couple hangout and enjoy each other

Husband's response: little response   he liked it   he

loved it

18. Appreciation night/party-decorate, have food and cake, involve the kids, make a banner

Husband's response: little response   he liked it   he loved it

19. Ask him what he wants you to pray about concerning him today. Let him know that you will be praying for him all day and keeping him lifted up

Husband's response: little response   he liked it   he loved it

20. Try a new love making position of his choice

Husband's response: little response   he liked it   he loved it

21. Role play or tell him what you fantasize about doing to him

Husband's response: little response   he liked it   he loved it

22. Send an email to close friends admiring your husband. Be sure to cc him on the email.

Husband's response: little response   he liked it   he loved it

23. Buy or make him a gift and include a love note

Husband's response: little response   he liked it   he loved it

24. Dress up for him. Get a manicure, pedicure, get hair done and let him know you did this with him in mind.

Husband's response: little response   he liked it   he loved it

25. Designate this as a "kill him with kindness" day. Ask him what you can do to help him out today. Are there any errands you can do for him? Allow him to watch TV uninterrupted and serve him dinner. Iron his clothes for the next day. Pack his lunch for tomorrow. Whatever you can do to show your husband acts of kindness, do it.

Husband's response: little response   he liked it   he loved it

26. Make a list of the top 10 reasons why you made a

good choice when you married him. You can place the list in a place where you know he will find it or you can present the list to him during your time alone with him.

Husband's response: little response   he liked it   he loved it

27. Encourage him to take a step in making his dream become a reality. If he wants to further his education, encourage him to sign up for an orientation course at the campus or look up classes online to get more information. If he wants to start his own business, encourage him to begin looking up the necessary requirements or schedule an appointment at a bank to discuss the possibility of getting a business loan.

Husband's response: little response   he liked it   he loved it

28. Serve him breakfast in bed

Husband's response: little response   he liked it   he loved it

29. Take him out to lunch.

Husband's response: little response   he liked it   he loved it

30. Ask him for 10 minutes of his time. During this time ask him if he needs your help in any area that would make his life easier. If he answers yes, be sure to allow him to tell you what he needs without your interruption, debates or opinions. Just listen and take notes.

Husband's response: little response   he liked it   he loved it

More Tips and Ideas

1. Greet him daily with a big smile, hug and kiss. Show him that you're excited that he is home. When a man enters the home of his mistress, she expresses enthusiasm. She doesn't act unconcerned.

2. Pray. Always invite God into your marital relationship. Your marriage will not succeed without God as the foundation.

3. Exercise to release endorphins

4. Show unconditional positive regard for your husband

5. Spend time with each other doing activities that your spouse picked out and enjoy it simply because you are with your spouse

6. Drink water, rest and eat well, take a multivitamin so your energy isn't drained which leads to moodiness and irritability

7. Date night 1 day/wk

8. Spend at least 30 minutes per day without the TV, kids and not talking about bills or other serious issues- Talk about dreams, how much you appreciate each other, massage each other, share a love letter

9. Remember the early days of dating and try to recreate those activities

10. Do things to "woe" the other person.

11. Tell your spouse in front of kids and others how much you appreciate your husband

12. Engage in sex-ting, provocative notes and follow through on your promises

13. Make out like you used to prior to marriage. Hide from the kids in the closet, bathroom or wherever to make out. Include kissing on the neck, ears and other places that turn your spouse on

14. Day of fun-all about having fun with your spouse and include activities, food, joking around

15. Watch a love story. Don't be offended if your husband isn't interested in this. Even if he is not interested, you can watch it alone. Women's minds seem to be in a loving mood after watching a sweet love story.

16. Learn to communicate your needs/wishes/desires without being critical of your spouse

17. Have sex often with the idea of putting your spouse first-focus on bringing pleasure to your spouse in everything you do

18. Caress and cuddle longer than usual

19. Have Valentine's Day more often. Bring romance back into the relationship.

20. Tell your spouse what you find attractive, irresistible about him-his style, the way he interacts

with the kids

21. Tell him your favorite body part of his is and why. Then make sure you take the opportunity to touch, rub against it or see it daily

22. Think sex. With all of the things we have to get accomplished in a day, it is easy to think about everything other than sex.

23. Agree on a time of the day that you feel most sexual and alternative between your time preferences and his time preferences

24. Tell him what turns you on or gets you in the mood for lovemaking

25. Plan a couple getaway

On any of day, sex is ALWAYS an option!

What I learned during this process of becoming my husband's mistress is, that as I ministered to him, I actually began seeing him differently. My desire to become his mistress began to be sincere. I cared about pleasing him. It rekindled the love and my desire for him.

Resources

Internet Resources: Christian based websites

http://www.thepurebed.com/

http://christiannymphos.org/

http://www.themarriagebed.com

http://www.covenantspice.com/index.html

http://www.familydynamics.net

http:// www.romancebetweenthelines.com

http://www.the-generous-husband.com

http://www.the-generous-wife.com

http:// www.howtogivehead.biz (Warning: This website is not Christian based and contains explicit, sexual and adult content)

Book Resources

The Lady, Her Lover and Her Lord by Bishop T.D. Jakes

Love and Respect by Dr. Emerson Eggrich

His Needs, Her Needs by Dr. William Harley Jr.

Being Good to Your Husband on Purpose by Becky

Hunter

A Wife After God's Own Heart by Elizabeth George

Intimate Issues by Lorraine Pintus and Linda Dillow

Becoming the Woman of His Dreams by Sharon Jaynes

10 Commandments of Marriage by Dr. Ed Young

Bibliography

Preface

1 http://www.love-sessions.com/cheating.htm

Who is the Mistress?

2 http://www.merriam-webster.com/dictionary/mistress.

Operate in Love

3 http://christianity.about.com/od/glossary/a/Agape.htm

Learn to Adapt

4 http://www.bing.com/Dictionary.

Importance of Encouragement

5 http://www.bing.com/Dictionary.

Comfort

6 http:// www.Mednet.com

7 http://psychcentral.com/lib/2008/about-oxytocin/

Admiration

8 http://www.thefreedictionary.com/admire

The Mistress is Drama Free

9 http://www.love-sessions.com/cheating.htm

K.I.S.S

10 http://www.acronymfinder.com/Keep-It-Short-%26-Simple-(KISS).html

Begin Bad in the bedroom

11 http://www.thefreedictionary.com/defiled

Be sexually adventurous with your husband

12 www.wikihow.com/Be-a—Mistress

All scripture quotations, unless otherwise indicated, are taken from
www.BibleGateway.com
Scripture quotations marked (AMP) are from The Holy Bible, Amplified Version
Scripture quotations marked (KJV) are taken from The Holy Bible, King James Version
Scripture quotations marked (NIV) are taken from The Holy Bible, New International Version
Scripture quotations marked (NKJV) are taken from The Holy Bible, New King James Version
Scripture quotations marked (ESV) are from The Holy Bible, English Standard Version

Other Titles by Dee Johnson

God's Girl: A Daily Word to Encourage Women to Live Out Their Purpose

Dee is a Published Author and Licensed Therapist that helps people work through and overcome life challenges. She lives in Houston TX with her husband Earnest and their two sons Jonathan and Jason.

You can learn more about Dee by visiting

www.FacingForwardOnline.org

You can also follow Author Dee Johnson on

Facebook at http://www.facebook.com/authordee.johnson

or

Twitter at https://twitter.com/Dee_Johnson2012

Made in the USA
Charleston, SC
21 January 2013